[Handwritten inscription:] Jim Dykes — Two meaningful syllables — reminders of a rich soul met in rural North Carolina. Thank you for the gift of your Self — Ken Hamilton

SoulCircling:
The Journey to the Who

Kenneth Hawley Hamilton, MD

Hope Healing Publications
P.O. Box 276
South Paris ME 04281-0276
(207) 743-9373

ISBN 0-9725760-0-2 (pbk.) $17.75

We are not human beings in search of a spiritual experience.
We are spiritual beings immersed in a human condition.

— Pierre Teilhard de Chardin

CONTENTS

Acknowledgments:

I dedicate this work to the memory of Earl Nightingale, who was such a great teacher of the psychology of human potential; to the memory of Barry Wood, M.D., whose soul still watches over me; to Sharon Williams, R.N., without whose gift of its name, H.O.P.E. would never have come into being; and to the hundreds of participants in H.O.P.E. group meetings who have demonstrated what it takes to discover health. I owe all of these wonderful people so much for my own development. This work expresses my deep gratitude to them all.

I am deeply grateful to those who have been close to me and lovingly scrutinized the development of Circling the Soul: Coming Home to Yourself ®: Laurie Cartier, Gus Jaccaci, Jim Mitchell, Barbara Sinclair, Susan Thompson, Jane Bamberg, and Bruce St. Thomas. We got a lot of pleasure out of circling our own souls, and we have delighted in bringing it to others.

I extend the same level of gratitude to Nikki Millonzi whose wonderful calligraphic symbol of SoulCircling graces the cover of this book.

I acknowledge the many people and their works that have helped me move from my early, purely masculine interpretation of God to the rich appreciation of the meaning of Father-Mother God. I shall use the word, God, throughout this work in the context of both genders. If I speak of a feminine aspect of God, I shall use the feminine pronouns. If I speak of a masculine aspect of God, I shall use the masculine pronouns. I shall also refer to God as It, not as an object, but as the source of both the masculine Father and the feminine Mother. This neutral form of the divine Source is, to me, the same as The Tao, Brahman, Ground of Being, and the God-head. I shall use these other names for God, and will capitalize them with the same awe and respect I have for The Name that has stayed with me since childhood. The Name has been my Friend since I was a child, for I knew then that God loved me.

Though I have always held God in awe, it would be many years before I realized that I could love God. When I came to that realization, I gave God a new name—Beloved. These personal names have great meaning for me, and I shall use them preferentially.

Many of the quotes in this work came to me without any identification of a copyright source. For the others, unless otherwise acknowledged, they have come from either The Columbia Dictionary of Quotations licensed from Columbia University Press © 1993; Correct Quotes from WordStar International Incorporated © 1990-92; Career Publishing, Inc. © 1969, 1972; Microsoft Bookshelf; or Bartlett's Familiar Quotations, 16th ed, Boston: Little, Brown, 1992.

The American Heritage® Dictionary of the English Language, now in its fourth edition, © 2000 by Houghton Mifflin Company, has been my favorite dictionary since it was first published in 1965. In its new edition, it now resides happily in my computer as well as on a shelf behind my shoulder. It has always nurtured my wordsmithing love of the inherent power of words.

Foreword

Here is a most timely book of rich rewarding wisdom; a work of prose poetry for the soaring of our souls. Now, when human conscious evolution is the emerging necessity of humanity and hangs daily in the balance of potential eternal defeat, now comes a new page in the history of the healing arts, and just in time. For here we learn that in our reunion with our souls is our salvation, our personal and social healing.

Here in the life and work of Dr. Ken Hamilton are inspiring stories of personal revelation and learning which lead to medical and spiritual medical and spiritual insights which, in turn, lead to a series of social inventions for personal and group healing. These inventions of H.O.P.E. groups and Soul Circles are pioneering examples of an evolutionary pathway up and out of our devolution and on to our human fulfillment and our divine destiny.

Ken Hamilton has come to his depth of insight wearing his soul on the outside as all great leaders do. He is willing to tell us the personal stories and crises through which he has passed from early childhood and throughout his maturing and his medical career. The reader is a witness to his struggles as well as his amazing healing revelations and subsequent adjustments and creations within his medical practice. We are privileged to have a close up view of an archetypal soul story. We also get full confirmation that the future of medicine is inevitably a soul-seeking enterprise. "In this time in human history, soul returns to our awareness as a guide to the truth", he writes. "Crisis is always an opportunity to listen to Spirit speak through your own soul....Virtually every practitioner of medicine has had such opportunities to open his or her awareness to the presence of soul. This process may well be a vital and necessary part of medical practice—the very heart of medicine."

Ken Hamilton goes on to establish many of the important phenomena now reemerging in the consciousness of the world culture to help describe and reconfirm the centrality of soul in our lives and our reasons for being. He uses personal stories, accounts from other doctors, writers and friends, and amazing narratives from anonymous members of H.O.P.E. groups to establish these phenomena. Thus, out of body experience, soul fragmentation due to trauma, near death experience, reincarnation, shamanic soul retrieval, and soul visitation become domains of contribution to the healthy, therapeutic and fulfilling understanding of soul.

Dr. Hamilton knows and demonstrates that this is truly a critical time of transformation in human culture. It is a time when the human species is required to take full responsibility for its own conscious evolution, for the creation of a global civilization of love and harmony and for the social architecture of a planetary renaissance. Sufficient to all those creative challenges, beyond the current dynamics of light, electricity and information, lies the healing dynamic of the human soul. The soul is the vessel of our salvation and our evolutionary triumph. Hamilton is one of the precious few among us who are the visionary voices and personal and social soul guides to open and tend the gates to the renaissance culture.

In this book, you will see the gatekeeper as prose-poet, the gatekeeper as medical doctor, the gatekeeper as inventive social scientist and entrepreneur, the gatekeeper as cosmological theologian and inspired preacher-teacher. In times of renaissance, when all the conceptual boundaries between domains of practice must dissolve and some among us must create and witness a new higher order synthesis of human potential and promise, here stands Ken Hamilton calling to us. Here he is offering us the soul-sharing social inventions of H.O.P.E. groups and Soul Circles. One hundred years ago Nicola Tesla formed the first dynamos for the generation of electricity; today here is Ken Hamilton inventing and forming the human dynamos of collective synergetic souls. From my experience of Ken's groups, I would describe their "output" as the soul collaborative creativity or the "soul creaticity" of human transcendence.

My friend Margaret Mead asked me to consider how to create scientific models which are organic and natural instead of arbitrary and man-made. She said the difference is in the intention. Arbitrary man-made models have as their intention the manipulation and control of people. Organic natural models have as their intention resonance and reverence. She would be proud and so am I of the medical and societal modeling and leadership of Dr. Kenneth Hamilton.

Welcome to the words of Ken Hamilton. Welcome to the heart and soul of Ken Hamilton. He is among the truly great sages of our time, brought to that place by the divine intervention and personal revelation he shows is our common heritage. He is brought to that place also by his unique doctoring and his healing service of life-long compassion.

Welcome to the reuniting of your egoic identity with your eternal soul.

August T. Jaccaci, November, 2002

Prologue: Eden, the Garden of Ego

Today, more and more people agree with Pierre Teilhard de Chardin's notion that every human is a spiritual being immersed in a human experience, rather than a human in search of a spiritual experience. I first heard the idea from Jacquelyn Small[1] in 1989 at a conference on addictions, and deep in my heart I knew it was true. For me, and I encourage you to look at your own experience, the only problem I have believing this is that my ego gets in the way— it needs so much to be in control. I sense that our egos have been doing this for countless centuries. There is a simple reason for this—our egos are very concrete about their business of keeping our survival interests in mind.

Evolutionary pressures created our complex, fight-or-flight survival response. When threatened, our spinal cord[2] screams, "Look out!" and our survival program kicks in, making us super-strong, super-fast, and super-intelligent. This remarkable program assures us the greatest chance of surviving any dangerous situation.

Our remarkable memories and our ability to actively seek and acquire knowledge enables us to keep track of the things that kicked off the response in the past and become alert for events that look like the old threat—not without inherent dangers, as we shall see.

With our acquired knowledge, we developed many other wonderful abilities, and many not so wonderful ones, especially the capacity to use the survival response to control others by making them afraid. Our capability to use knowledge includes the aptitude for misapplying[3] it.

We have a long history of the use and abuse of knowledge; reaching back to before the early humanoid we call Neanderthal Man. We uncovered his skeleton in a cave in the Neander River valley in Germany in 1856. His bones were many thousands of years old, and before long, other Neanderthal bones led us to decide that the species was over 100,000 years old. Neanderthals were resourceful, fire- and tool-using, cave-dwelling people who survived several serious ice ages. Nevertheless, they were not our immediate ancestors.

About 30,000 yeas ago, a new human appeared whose bones were first found in Cro-Magnon, France, so we called the new one Cro-Magnon Man. These people were more intelligent, more skilled than the Neanderthals—a better survivor—and the Neanderthals then simply disappeared. Cro-Magnon humans are our ancestors. They are we.

We increased our knowledge, as Homo sapiens, the knowing human, is wont to do. After about 20,000 years as nomadic hunter-gatherers, we, the Cro-Magnons, learned to domesticate plants and animals, so we did not have to spend so much time chasing our food around. Now we were able to stay in one place and build simple hut-homes to protect ourselves from the elements. We were learning.

However, after only about 2,500 years of this new life style, we began to build fortified communities with heavy walls and towers. We were putting our knowledge to use to defend ourselves from others who were putting their knowledge to use to attack us! We were beginning to use our knowledge not only to put property to use but also to take it away from other humans…. We were stealing from ourselves! We had begun to misapply our knowledge for the purpose of attacking and defending ourselves. It seems we have misused the knowledge of good and evil for only about 7,500 years.

Over that time, while we were developing technologies of murder on the one hand, we managed to develop remarkable civilizations and wonderful technologies on the other. We became technicians, artisans, and artists. We became musicians, composers, actors, and playwrights. We created things of beauty ranging from paintings to symphonies to pyramids. Clearly, as we developed the ability to destroy, we developed the ability to create—what an incredible contrast!

Our social development led us to develop insights into our behavior, and we became poets and philosophers. We questioned how it was possible that we could have learned to be so destructive. Insight showed us that our knowledge was the source of all of our power. We did not know how we had gotten this great power, but our ability to harm each other told us that it had to be a mistake of God in which somehow all of us had taken part. The storytellers of the children of Israel figured it out and their account of how it happened is the Legend of the Garden of Eden.

The legend is a remarkable history of the ego. In it, even God has one! The story belongs to all of us through the millennia in which we developed our knowledge; so, you can appreciate the Eden story of Genesis 3 paraphrased in contemporary language:

Genesis 3:

This Supreme Being called God, having just used the power of His knowledge to create the Earth, the Sun, the Moon, and the Stars, needed somebody to tell Him what a good job He had done, so He made a man in His image to talk to Him and a woman to keep the man company. He wanted them close to Him, so He put them in the prettiest spot on His World where he also kept his stash of Knowledge, disguised as a tree. Because Knowledge was so powerful, it was dangerous beyond belief, and he didn't want the man and the woman to have it.

However, there was this smart character in the garden called Serpent, whom God had made, but who didn't like God. He figured that he could make a lot of profit at God's expense by talking the man and the woman into eating some of God's stash of Knowledge. One day, when God wasn't looking, Serpent stole some fruit off the tree. He took it to the woman because he knew he could talk her into eating it and that she, in turn, could talk the man into eating it.

Prologue

It happened just as Serpent planned, but God figured out what had happened. He got mad at all three of them and punished them for their disobedience. He told them he was done with them and they were going to have to get out of the Garden. He cut off the serpent's arms and legs making it crawl on its belly forever after. He told the man that he'd have to work painfully hard in the fields to grow food for him and the woman. He told the woman that she was going to have to bear children, who would cause her great physical pain in childbirth and great emotional pain in raising them.

To make matters even worse, he told them if they ever tried to come back, there would be armed guards at the gate to keep them out and a shining, spinning sword over the gate that would slice them to pieces if they managed to get past the guards. He was just that mad at them. He's God, so He never forgets, and He never goes back on His word....

We've been out on our own ever since.

The story of the Garden of Eden took centuries of polishing in thousands of campfire repetitions before we had the skill with which to write it down in about 750 BCE. It lays blame, guilt, and punishment on us through a shameful belief that the divine Source of our lives, God, has rejected us. The Eden story is as much with us today as ever... perhaps even more so in view of the murderous technologies that we have developed with the knowledge we believe we got from God against His will.

If we don't change those beliefs, we are doomed to misapply that knowledge until we have destroyed the world. There is a star-born presence in each of us—our *soul*—that has everything we need to be able to make that change. This book is all about discovering that *stellar presence.*

The *content* of this work is a *psychology...* as long as we remember that the root meaning of "psychology" is *the study of the soul*. This study reveals the way in which the eternal, spiritual soul works in partnership with the ephemeral, secular ego to create every human life. This collaboration reveals the vital need for the ego to recognize the presence of the soul and allow itself to integrate into the soul.

The work of integrating the ego and the soul is a process that heals us. I offer you the idea that this healing enables us to change our problems into our possibilities. My name for this process is *homecoming*. Homecoming gives us hope of finding meaning, value, and purpose in our lives. We can make this profound and joyful shift because the Godhead made us the most diverse and creative species the world has ever known. He also did something else that all of the prophets know and understand extremely well—imbued in us the ability to become aware of our spiritual nature.

We are born spiritual, remembering God. By about the age of five, most of us have forgotten who and what we really are, just like the three-year-old girl of the popular story who was heard to ask her new-born brother, "Tell me about God; I'm beginning to forget." I told that story in a public talk and a woman in the audience made an appointment to see me shortly thereafter. She told me that her son had been telling her things like, "When I was in heaven…" and "Before I came here, God told me…" as soon as he could talk. She had always put him down for this "crazy talk", but now she was going to apologize and encourage him to keep those memories. How many children do you know who talk like that?

Contemporary society has forgotten how to remind us of this wonderful, vital aspect of our nature that knows God personally. Indeed, most of our institutions, including our contemporary religions, spend a great deal of energy denying our spiritual nature, thanks to thinking that rose 600 years ago out of the feudal, dispirited Dark Ages to begin a secular movement toward classicism and humanism that we call The Renaissance—the *re-birth* of our creative, artistic nature.

Over the next 300 years, the physical universe showed us how to take it apart and measure it… and we fell in love with it. This new passion marked the beginning of what we call today

"The Enlightenment". Its rational child, the Age of Reason, led us to believe we were forcing the universe (God) to reveal more of its secret stash of knowledge than just good and evil. We believed we were using that knowledge to take power back from God and be able to control It. Geniuses like René Descartes, Isaac Newton, Galileo, and Copernicus were all part of this great expansion of knowledge.

Descartes' rationalist thinking, summarized as, "I think, therefore I am," made the body-mind all-powerful. Rationalism rejected the soul, and even fought the Vatican's claim to the existence of our spirit. The success of rationalism was a major victory for our species' ego. Reason, and its stepchild, science, became the Way to the Truth. We did not need a Creator to get this universe going. We used our collective species-ego to describe how our universe worked in apparently random, accidental, and inanimate patterns without any intelligence to guide it.

This is how we got about as far away from the Garden as we can safely get... much farther and we destroy the Garden and ourselves. We must head toward home; it is time to remember *who* and *what* we really are—spiritual beings called souls living in ego-directed human bodies. The time has come to learn how to bring our egos, our secular centers, into partnership with our souls, our spiritual centers. Let us learn to support others as they seek their own centers. As we do, we shall help each other find out what our souls came here to do. We shall discover the nature of our covenant with God so talked about in the scripture of the Faith Family religions.

It is time for us to learn how to be Human Beings. We have to learn to wander through the fields of human endeavor knowing that we did not steal them from the Source of everything but that they are divine gifts of infinite variety. We need only to look into their wondrous variety to find the songs of our individual souls. We can then listen to that song with our hearts, singing and dancing it—following the inspiring call of a muse[4]. The more we sing and dance this song, the more our souls come to share their experience of the physical universe with the spiritual universe. In this way, the Creator comes to know the finite soul-part of Its eternal and infinite Self.

I, like many of you who read this, had to find out the hard way that the ego is limited. Remembering the spiritual encounters of my childhood has helped me wake my ego to the presence of my soul and bring the two together in my own homecoming. I will teach you how to recognize your soul, your spiritual center, and hold onto it in this world of rapid change. Souls come to human life for good reasons, and we shall explore what those reasons might be. I will show you the process of "circling" your soul, which will give you insights into your spiritual self. These insights will lead you toward your lovely soul song[5]. Circling your soul is both a process and a practice. As you move through it you will become proficient in working with others, and you will learn to recognize the difference between ego-based relationships and soul-based relationships. When minds work together, their output exceeds their individual capabilities in separation—a process called *synergy*. When souls collaborate, they create super-synergy. You will discover the delight of creating your own SoulCircle support group, in which you hold each other's life in light, hope, and love, and find meaning and wellness for yourself.

When you have come home, join me in rewriting the legend of the Garden of Eden.

Introduction: A surgeon sheathes his scalpel

Here you are with this book in your hands. Why have you chosen to pick it up?

Are you curious to learn something more about the nature of the soul—yours in particular? Have you been in touch with it lately? Would you like to become more familiar with it? You have come to a resource for help in finding the answers—answers that lie inside of you, ready for you to find them.

What does it mean to "circle" your soul? And what is "the journey to the who"? What might a doctor know about the soul, and why he has taken the time to develop his acquaintance with it? The answers are all here.

Let me tell you now about the way in which the Mystery of the Universe revealed Itself to me, changing my life forever.

In 1975, I was struggling with anger, not knowing that it was mine. I complained to my practice manager that I thought the world was angry with me. His response was to offer me the loan of a Nightingale-Conant[6] *INSIGHT* audiotape that he had received a week before. He told me that he thought it addressed my concern. In it, Earl Nightingale, radio personality, author, and co-founder of the Nightingale-Conant Corporation, talked about a variation of the Law of Returns[7] that he called the Law of Correspondence. Simply stated, it says that the attitudes you sense in the world around you are reflections of and correspond precisely to the attitudes that you project into that world. Earl went on to say that we choose all of our attitudes (even though we may have forgotten why we made the choice in the first place); so we can choose another to replace the one that is not working well any more.

I was in a crisis over the anger. I had to make another choice, and when I found myself in a familiar, anxious situation where the anger would come up, I encouraged myself to "take it easy," repeating it over and over in the face of the anxiety that led to the anger. The effect was immediate… and I knew the meaning of "Physician, heal thyself!"

I subscribed to the monthly *INSIGHT* tape series and discovered a great resource for my own development. Coincidentally, every new tape seemed to bring helpful ideas I could share with those patients who wanted more than an operation. They clearly benefited from their vicarious studies of what I came to call "the psychology of success." They recovered very quickly from their operations and got out of hospital with record short stays. This psychology had no direct correlation to the "bedside psychology" I had learned in medical school, so I had to take time to see if it really worked. After ten years of its study and application, I knew I had to take a critical look at conventional therapeutic psychology. Rather than leave my surgical practice for two years in a graduate program, I chose to study under a tutor, and my intention led me to Barry Wood, M.D., a gifted psychiatrist in a nearby city.

He was a wonderful mentor. Over the next year, we developed a rich, productive relationship. He had a deep, rich reserve of valuable experiences, including extensive work with the "Twelve-step" recovery programs of Alcoholics Anonymous. He sensed my own recovery needs and suggested that I became an active participant in that part of the twelve-step program that focused on helping Adult Children of Alcoholics recover from family patterns of addiction (which I did not realize were present in my family). I followed his recommendation and the experience proved to be instrumental in what was to follow.

Our relationship deepened in many ways when he found he had incurable cancer. While he was still in hospital after the emergency abdominal surgery that diagnosed the illness, he was given a copy of Bernie Siegel's *Love, Medicine and Miracles*[8]. Bernie's experiences and knowledge fascinated Barry and he connected with Bernie shortly after getting home from the hospital. When Barry and I came together again, he arranged for Bernie and me to meet.

That meeting took place at one of Bernie's workshops called *The Psychology of Illness and the Art of Healing.* I also found Bernie's work fascinating, and I commented on it to the hosts of the workshop who told me about the similar work of Jerry

Jampolsky, M.D. who would be giving a workshop one month later; so I signed up on the spot!

Both Jerry and Bernie were working with medical/surgical patients in support groups. Barry's experience with non-medical 12-step recovery support groups became the third element in discovering the miraculous potential humans have when they join their minds in a shared intention.

Three months later, five of my cancer patients clearly had the potential to be able to support each other's lives in the face of their illnesses. I asked them if they would like to start a support group for each other. We came together for the first time on February 12, 1987, and chose our name—HOPE. At the next meeting, we made our name an acronym for Healing Of Persons Exceptional. "Healing" was synonymous with wholeness, health, and holiness; "persons" signified our common human-ness; and "exceptional" reflected our wondrous diversity.

Because of the lethal potential of cancer, death of some group members was inevitable; so I knew that I needed to learn about the growing hospice movement. Moreover, one name in the hospice movement kept cropping up—Elisabeth Kübler-Ross, M.D.[9]—and I knew I would get to know her and her work in much the same way that I had met Bernie and Jerry. You can imagine my surprise and delight when a brochure for one of her workshops called, "*Life, Death, and Transition*" appeared shortly after. I signed up for it without paying much attention to its content. It turned out not to be about hospice work, but about healing the traumas that life could bestow on a human! Had I read the brochure carefully, I most certainly would not have gone. Had I not gone, I doubt that I would be writing this book today, for it was in the context of the workshop that The Mystery revealed itself to me!

The workshop took place in an old Shaker village fifty miles from where I live… and what an wonderfully appropriate place for this meeting it was! Whereas many of my patients had told me about their traumas in life, I never asked them to go into detail. Here were eighty-five people going deeply into the gruesome experiences of their suffering... it tore me apart. Hearing these stories touched me to my core and I began to grieve at a depth I had never before experienced, or even knew was possible.

After two days of almost non-stop grieving, I woke at dawn to find my pillow wet with tears. I knew I had to go walking with my intense feelings of sadness, so I dressed quietly and stole out of the room past my sleeping roommates. I took with me my Sony Walkman and a tape with the mystical Grateful Dead song, *Ripple*, which we sang to open our H.O.P.E. Group meetings. Stepping out of the dormitory, I met a gray, misty morning. I wandered around the lanes of the old settlement, *Ripple* playing softly in my ears. I soon found my way down the lane that led to the community cemetery with its single gravestone with the word "Shaker" on it. Halfway there, and right next to a full-size wooden sculpture of the crucified Jesus, I was aware of a presence in the mist beyond a gap in a stone wall—it was my mother, and she had died ten years before!

She was sitting still, looking gently at me with her remarkable, yellow-brown eyes… just looking. Without giving a thought to this seemingly unnatural phenomenon, I said to her, "Mom, I love you, and thanks for waiting. You're free to go." Her eyes, which I remember so well for the deep sorrow always within them, brightened and were the center of a smile that seemed to encompass her whole being. With this smile, she gave thanks for the gift of love from the son who could never before tell her that he loved her. Free, she swished away into the morning mist.

Now, something to my left got my attention. There, in the same mist was a human outline in black, looking as if someone had drawn it on the whiteness of the mist with a piece of charcoal. I knew it was my father, twenty years dead. Behind him was another outline of exactly the same shape… his father (they looked like brothers). I said to my father, "Dad, I love you and I've always loved you. Thank you for waiting. You're free to go." As I said these words to a father who could never talk about love, I saw a black cord that stretched from my heart through his heart to his father's heart. It begin to glow cherry-red. The glow became brighter and brighter, finally becoming yellow-white, at which magical instant, it burned! And these two images swished away into the mist.

In that instant, I felt a deep, deep peace come over me. I felt as if some great power had lifted a huge weight from my shoulders. I floated the whole way back to my room. I showered and changed in the comfort of that peace, and enjoyed a delicious breakfast. When the work began later that morning, I wept no more. I felt the pain and the suffering, but no longer suffered myself. I sensed then that my parents had suffered in their youth, and I had somehow taken on their suffering. The pain had ended with that simple, beautiful moment of love, compassion, and forgiveness that I had experienced with their souls in that early morning mist.

As the day of peace wore on, I knew I had to tell the others what had happened to me that morning. I had not taken my turn "on the mat" telling my story, and it seemed that the time for the story had not been right until that evening, the last evening of the work. I told the story in full reference to what had happened early that morning. My facilitator commented, "Elisabeth calls that divine intervention." I responded with a silent nod, fully aware that I had had a profoundly spiritual encounter and that some part of me could rest after many years of defensive actions.

Tomorrow would be a day of celebration with a visit from Elisabeth, herself, that would end with an evening of skits, poetry, and songs by the participants. I knew I had to sing *Ripple* for them, so I found the "MC" of the skits and asked if he had an opening for a karaoke. He said, "Okay, you'll be number nine, and that'll be the last." I retired to my bed with a wonderful sense of being whole, helped by knowing that I had all Thursday afternoon in which to prepare my performance of *Ripple*.

Thursday dawned bright and clear; so I began in earnest to develop my gift to everyone there. I danced and sang when and where I could in private, away from everyone else. By that afternoon, I had it, and I was as high as a kite from the repetition of the song and its dance. I heard a voice inside of me say, "You've got to ask the dancers their opinion of your dance." "The Dancers" were the Shakers who used to dance to attain altered states of consciousness, as they describe in their hymn, Simple Gifts. I was to go down the lane past the crucified Jesus to the Shaker cemetery with its single stone. There, I was to go in and share my song and dance with the inhabitants of that holy ground.

I walked down the lane, listening to *Ripple* as I had done the day before. This time, though, was all together different... the sky was Canadian blue, the air moved softly, and the maple trees glowed in the peak of their autumn colors. As I turned to face the latched cemetery gate, I saw a smiling face in every maple leaf in the dozen trees in front of me—the souls of the many inhabitants. Aloud, I asked, "I have a song and dance I'd like your opinion on. May I come in, please?" The smiles broadened... knowing I was welcome, I reached for the gate latch.... When my hand was still a foot away from the latch, it moved back and the gate opened wide—I had not touched it!

I heard my voice say in wonder, "It opened all by itself!"

Being ever so welcome, I entered. I sang my song and danced my dance for this space full of souls. I felt a warm acceptance, a deep gratitude, and a deep, inner peace. I felt a graceful presence holding me in its gentle embrace, and experienced the immense joy of knowing that I was loved by a power far greater than mine.

I backed out of the cemetery and pulled the gate shut as I left. It was very hard to close because I had to force the latch back against the gate in order for it to clear its steel notch bolted into the granite gatepost! What had opened it?

As I turned to go back up the lane, I realized that it was the first of October—the fifty-fourth anniversary of the day in which I took my first breath! Happy Birthday, Kenneth!

Today, I wear a brass belt buckle I had cut from a blank in the shape of the word, "SOAR." People often comment on it, and then I tell them two things about me that both satisfy and pique their curiosity. First, I tell them that it reminds me of my soaring experiences in a beautiful, white, long-winged glider from 1967 through 1981. These motorless, soaring flights lasted as long as eight hours, went as far as 200 miles, and climbed as high as 24,700 feet! Second, I tell them that today I soar longer, farther, and higher than I ever did in that glider as I help people discover their soul's journey through H.O.P.E. Groups and SoulCircling.

When I had this transforming experience in Alfred, people in other Maine cities and towns had already heard about H.O.P.E. and they had begun calling on me to help start groups in their towns. The next spring, a group in a city two hours away from where I worked called me to start a group there, and I knew I had to choose between H.O.P.E. and my surgical practice. H.O.P.E. was taking a lot of my time, and in spite of the highly competent backup provided by my two busy colleagues, I felt I was compromising my availability to my surgical patients. I also saw that H.O.P.E. could be a great benefit to all of the caring professions and those they served.

I was moving on, changing my hard-earned career of surgically treating disease into a career of nurturing health and wellness. The following Spring, I submitted my resignation from the active surgical staff effective six months later and set up the not-for-profit H.O.P.E. 501(c)(3) organization. When my resignation became effective on November 1, I set out to find H.O.P.E. a home where I could also work in my new specialty of counseling and stress management. Within one week, the vice president of a local trust company called me, asking if H.O.P.E. would be interested in having the use of a lovely Victorian house whose deceased owners had directed the trust to use it for health-related purposes! They asked me to submit a proposal in H.O.P.E.'s name, and rewarded H.O.P.E. with the home it now shares with six practitioners of complementary health care[10].

In 1990, I reached a peak of guiding seven H.O.P.E. Group meetings a week. Some of the H.O.P.E. Group members asked if I would teach them how to guide groups, and we worked out a training program. Their groups were successful, too—the process could be replicated.

From the outset, participants described the H.O.P.E. process as "spiritual." The focus on hope developed motives for discovering meaning, value, and purpose in their lives. This discovery helped people heal, although it might not have cured them of their disease. (We will discuss this distinction later.) We saw that healing was a unique, spiritual process for everyone, celebrating his or her exceptional nature. We also saw that everyone, persons all, could find the process for him- or her- self.

We came to see each life as the journey of a soul, and to understand that H.O.P.E.'s work was to help people find their soul's purpose. That discovery was a coming home to their truth. We refined the group process into a workshop format, and called this homecoming "Circling the Soul: Coming Home to Yourself"®. H.O.P.E.'s group work and SoulCircling workshops transform people's lives.

Many have asked me to write about H.O.P.E. and SoulCircling. It has been a delight to be able to respond to them..

I have divided my response into three parts:

Part One opens with a look at the history of the universe and our world, and how we got to where we are today. It then examines the ego, the soul, and the psychology that describes their relationship. It describes homecoming in detail, and it emphasizes how awareness of the presence of the soul is vital to the achievement of success.

Part Two contains a detailed description of the process that opens the dialog between the ego and the soul—SoulCircling. It contains specific exercises to enable you to work the entire process. It also tells you how to create a powerful support group to help you on your journey.

Part Three offers a consideration of the potential that lies in front of us… the soul journey of our human race.

Part 1: Two vital parts of self: ego and soul.

Man has falsely identified himself with the pseudo-soul or ego. When he transfers his sentence of identity to his true being, the immortal Soul, he discovers that all pain is unreal. He no longer can even imagine the state of suffering.

Paramahansa Yogananda

The American Heritage® Dictionary of the English Language defines Self as "1) The total, essential, or particular being of a person; the individual; 2) The essential qualities distinguishing one person from another; individuality; 3) One's consciousness of one's own being or identity; ego." However, see for yourself that "self" has two components: ego and soul.

Ego is a finite part of self that utilizes its perceptions of life to make judgments of situations and critically decide how to respond to those situations. It works separately from others, using relationships expediently to achieve its purposes. It uses its genetic, ephemeral gifts of form, temperament[11], talent, and intelligence, and the acquired, finite gifts of the environment to plot and scheme its own, special way through life, searching for a spiritual experience… without any knowledge of what comprises such an experience.

The soul is an infinite part of self that comes into each of us from eternity… time without beginning or end. It immerses itself in the ego's inventory to join other souls in service to each other and to the divine Source of all life.

The soul knows the lines along which the ego will develop. It works to help the ego develop the strengths that can help the self find the greatest power of the Universe, love. It sets up crises in which the ego will have the opportunity to recognize the soul's presence. It knows that circumstances will likely force it to fragment itself, and perhaps even to leave the body temporarily while the body's basic survival mechanisms take over. It knows how to heal these traumas and bring the ego into collaboration with it.

19

The soul sees this collaboration, this working together as a spiritual relationship and uses it to move toward love, the fire of creation—the success path of life. The collaboration of the ego and the soul is a partnership that fulfills the meaning of life. It is a coming home.

Chapter 1: In the beginning…

This among humankind I have seen:
A long life lived to itself withdrawn;
Upon its features written, broken dreams,
Cracked like the black mud beneath the sun.

This among humankind I have seen:
A life long to God and others drawn;
Upon its features, dreams yet unborn:
New life earth-cracking upwards to the sun.
—Terry Hemingway

Principles:

- You and I have been promised these lives from the beginning of time.
- That beginning was no accident, and neither are we.

In the Beginning:

Have you ever wondered where you came from and how you seem to know certain things without ever being told about them? I bet you have, but if you are like me, when I asked my mother those things she passed them off by saying, "Go ask your father." My father then said, "Hmmm, that's kind of a silly question." End of conversation.

Well, Human, you and I have been here since the beginning of time. It makes no difference whether time began with the cracking of the Cosmic Egg, Genesis 1:1, or the Big Bang. They all describe exactly the same thing—the creation of the Universe. They all use different words and symbols because we have not yet been able to agree on how this marvelous Creation came to be.

I shall use symbols of the "Big Bang" theory throughout this chapter because they have held my fancy since my teens, when

I first encountered the growing body of evidence that the universe was expanding from a point of light. In 1950, Fred Hoyle, the astronomer and mathematician who did not accept this theory, derisively called this grand expansion of light a "big bang". Ironically, the name stuck—a workable name for the greatest adventure of all time.

We did not have these human bodies when The Adventure began about fifteen billion years ago, but It promised them to us then. The proportions of matter and antimatter and the relationships of the resulting atomic and subatomic particles themselves guaranteed this outcome. Our bodies and the lives they live are the gift of a Life infinitely greater than you or I—a perfect, pure intention rising out of an indescribable void and uttering its only commandment: "Be!"

"Be!" is a perfect, eternal thought encompassing a perfect, infinite body in a single point of light. Like all points, it has but one dimension—and this one includes all time and space. It is both eternal and infinite. In the glorious instant of Its becoming, that Holy Thought, that Incredible Speck, expanded Its light into all of the dimensions of time and space and joyously cried out, "I am!" That passionate cry echoes yet from the farthest reaches of the universe. We are those echoes.

According to Big Bang theory, this Incredible Speck of Light, in the first instant of being[12] inflated at an unimaginable rate... a trillion, trillion times in the tiniest fraction of the first second of all time. That brilliant speck expanded far faster than the speed of light, at a rate just slow enough to keep it from blowing apart into a faint, dissipating cloud of gas and just fast enough to keep it from collapsing back in on itself. If either had happened, neither of us would be here to talk about it. The odds for this to have happened at just the right speed are incredibly minute! Our beautiful universe must be part of a great idea.

At the end of the inflation of the Incredible Speck of Light, when some cooling had taken place, and before the first second had yet passed, the first particles—quarks and electrons—appeared. They were a chaotic quark-electron stew. When the Incredible Speck was but three minutes old, the first hydrogen atoms appeared. It took the next ten thousand years to turn all of the electrons and quarks into hydrogen, which is still the most common element in the universe. The hydrogen came together in giant clouds with gravity enough to compress themselves into massive balls that burned the hydrogen into helium. This atomic change released light and heat. Today, we call these glowing bodies "stars."[13]

The biggest stars developed so much heat and pressure that they blew themselves apart. Their unbelievable internal pressures crushed the helium and hydrogen together in a myriad of fascinating combinations. In this way, Light put together all of the elements we know today. This expansion of Light produced what we can truly call "stardust," the stuff of which our planet and we are made.

The precision required to get all of this "just right" is so great that astrophysicists have calculated that the odds for this to be a chance happening are 10^{40}(ten to the fortieth power) to one, which is one trillion times one trillion times one trillion times ten thousand to one!

In order to create a planet with the rocky continents, the watery oceans, and an oxygen-containing atmosphere necessary for life, stardust has to gather in just the right amounts in specific relationships to special kinds of stars. It apparently takes a family of planets to make it possible for one of them to be able to create complex life. The odds of this happening by accident are miniscule—as small as the chance of the Expansion happening at just the right speed. Yet, this particular arrangement has to have happened millions of times throughout this immeasurably huge universe[14].

That "10^{40}" number shows up again in the odds that water, salts and ammonia can come together in a random way to form a single cell capable of replicating itself. Biophysicists threw lightning bolts at warm water enriched with salt and ammonia for a long time, and succeeded in creating some new, but simple, molecules with but the tiniest fraction of the complexity needed to make self-replicating cells. So it seems that the odds against either of us being here by accident may well be as low as a googol to one, or 1 in 10^{100} (one in ten to the one hundredth power)... a number greater than the total number of atoms in the universe!

The people calculating these odds are reputable scientists in the well-established fields of astrophysics and biology. Scientists exploring other seemingly accidental relationships in the Universe have found special fixed numbers called "constants" to describe these relationships. Now they find that if these numbers were off by the tiniest percentage, the Universe could never have given birth to stars, let alone us humans. We are coming to realize that we are all here on this pale blue dot in the face of what are, quite literally, astronomical odds. We are certainly not accidents.... We are a part of the Intention to Be!

You, me, every tree, every bird, every cloud, every river, every rock *are* because of the wondrous, beautiful Intention arising from deep in the void to be with us through all time. That Intention was there in the Awesome Inflation and Expansion, the sound of which was no "bang" but that of *joyous laughter* as The Creator began the greatest adventure ever.

We are more than just the atoms that comprise our bodies. We have minds to think with, and we use our thoughts to create intentional actions and ideas. When we focus sharply and clearly for a long enough time on any thought or idea, we can create physical things.[15]

Our growing realization of the pure potential of the Universe helps us to know that nothing is impossible. Look at what minds have created. All things, whether divine or secular, were once pure thoughts. Questions that analyze Divine thought—Truth—cannot threaten it; it simply is. Questions threaten secular thought because it lacks the integrity of Truth. Throughout recorded history, we have demonstrated our ability to choose the spiritual path. We have also displayed our ability to get lost in secular thinking. We need help with our choices.

The Great Invocation[16] opens with the expression, "From the point of light in the mind of God...." Though Alice Bailey wrote this years before Fred Hoyle coined his famous phrase, it speaks of how the Great Expansion began, and still goes on within God's mind—sacred thought. If our minds move, store, and combine information, so must God's mind, for we are made in God's image, are we not? Does it not make sense that the mind of God encompasses Its entire creation? Does it not make sense that God needs to know what goes on in Its body—the physical universe?

Thought must connect all of the pieces of the universe. It must be able to move between them without any of the temporospacial limits of the physical universe. Indeed, several exquisite quantum physical experiments have demonstrated that information moves virtually instantaneously between those incredibly tiny first particles, electrons and photons, regardless of the distance between them[17]. These experiments suggest that thought carries this information as if space and time do not exist!

We have discussed and debated the relationship between the mind and the brain for hundreds of years—as long as we have believed that thought was somehow related to the brain. As science has become more skilled at focusing on the physiological functioning of the brain, it has identified many chemical substances related to specific processes of thought. As a result, some scientists have brazenly concluded that thought originates in the chemical processes of the brain. Their thesis makes the creative mind secondary to the created body. Apparently, they never believed that all action proceeds out of thought—"in the beginning was the Word." They put the cart in front of the horse; these chemical processes act only in response to thought! The quantum physics experiments mentioned above, coupled with some later thought experiments, suggest that a mental universe encompasses the physical universe. The poet and mystic, William Blake (1757-1827) said, "My brain is an organ that my mind finds useful."

Our creativity identifies our species. What moves us to think creatively? Money? Luxury? Greed? Survival of the fittest? Fame? Some might reply "all of the above." However, do these answers actually explain our dreams of going to the stars? Explain why we fabricate great telescopes with which to penetrate the stellar mystery. Explain why we create spaceships that have already taken us to the moon and that someday will take us to the stars.

Nothing stimulates our creativity as much as passion. What else could have kept Tom Edison on track through almost ten thousand failed attempts to make that first incandescent electric bulb. Greed? Edison could have satisfied greed a lot easier than by burning up ten thousand filaments, so I think not! Money? He could have made money a lot more easily than by stubbornly sweating over each filament design. But then, he was the person who said, "Success is one percent inspiration and ninety-nine percent perspiration." What motivates a man to put out that much sweat? What motivates us to explore space and explain its mysteries? Passion fuels the fires of our engines of curiosity and creation.

God's passion creates and sustains that wondrous Point of Light. That passion remains with us, undiminished, in our atoms. It is a gift of the stars... memories calling us back to their birthplace.

Passion is a matter of the soul, not the mind, or the body. It has a profound influence on both. Passion leads us to seek enjoyment: to engage in joyful behaviors. Joyous laughter is not unique to humans. We learned it from God. The sound of the Great Expansion is certainly God's joyous laughter. When we laugh, we increase the amount of beta-endorphins and interferons in our brains and spinal cords, we feel good, and we give our immune systems a big boost. Serenity, inner peace, and bliss all have relationships to joy, and have direct, beneficial effect on the chemicals that turn on and regulate the immune system—our greatest protection against bacterial infections, viral infections (including HIV) and cancers. Laughter is, indeed, the best medicine, and a smile is a wonderful umbrella on those gloomy days that rain on the soul.

The passion of the Universe frames everything that we think, feel, and do, with but one exception—fear. Fear is not of the Universe. Fear is the product of our agile minds working as if God were standing on the moon, stroking Its hoary chin, bemused by the sight of this mob of two-leggeds running around Its world, wondering how such a strange accident could have happened in Its universe. If God feared anything for even the tiniest instant, it would be fearfully projecting its defenses all over the place, and the only "constant" would be confusion. The wondrous expansion would have been flawed and could not have sustained itself. However, it happened as it did because God's joyous song makes both God and Its universe whole.

For thousands of years we have been thinking and acting by projection. We project forward into unknown future time based on our projections into past time that no longer exists. Thus, we create fearful, life-threatening scenarios that become real because thought leads to action. We create anger from our fear, and use it to defend ourselves, believing that the best defense is a good offense. Consequently, we attack the object of our fear by throwing everything at it from thoughts to hydrogen bombs. Indeed, anger is another form of projection, a tragic stepchild of fear. The time has come for us to stop throwing ourselves all over time and space. God has already fed us the knowledge to know that the Point of Light in Its Mind promises each of us the time and space we occupy here and now.

As we have God's body, mind, and soul within us, so must we have God's spirit within us. The divinely fundamental spirit in each of us is as intangible as the breath. We in the West are now discovering—with the help of our science—how the spirit of God expresses itself. God's spirit expresses itself in perfect relationship with the whole universe. Our spirit reflects God's spirit back at God. This relationship manifests the essence of love.

Based on the above, three more points will close this chapter:

First, we are all equal, meaning that no one of us has the right to exercise power over anyone else because s/he is a "lesser being." We are all Mind, Body, Soul, and Spirit. They are ours only because their Source is the Creation, Itself.

Second, all human beings are different. Our bodies, temperaments, passions, and experiences are all different. No two of us are alike, including identical twins[18]. Even they have differences—differences of the soul.

Third, like God, we are also Light, Life, Love, and Laughter, which make us equal in the eyes of God. We can maintain that equality in our own eyes.

Now a simple question based on this awareness: "What did God put each one of us here to do?"

In addition, one more question out of the first: "What was God's purpose in creating our wonderfully diverse and creative species?

My experience tells me that we find the answers when we open a dialog between the ego and the soul. So let us go and visit the ego first and then the soul and ask each of them that question.

Chapter 2: Ego, the Navigator of the Ship of Life—the Seeker.

Principles:

- The ego comes here *in* our DNA--the source of all elements of our personality.
- Our ego strengths help us find our way through life.
- The ego, without a spiritual balance, is the source of *all* of our harmful behaviors.

What is the ego?

My earliest recollection of the word, ego, goes back to seventh grade, and my first Latin class with Sir Hayes. The Latin words he taught us then were *ego sum*, meaning I am.

Later, I discovered I had an ego. It was ME… what I thought about myself, what others felt about me, what I had, and what I could achieve. Looking back on my life, I have become aware that my ego was certainly not the who of my life but the what of it. My ego had physical properties of size and strength, as I might have heard a family member say, "Toby (my childhood nickname), you have a strong ego," or "Your Uncle Alex certainly had a big ego!"

Medical school taught me to define the ego as "that portion of the human personality experienced as the 'self' or 'I' which perceives, remembers, evaluates, plans, and in other ways is responsive to and acts in the surrounding physical and social world."[19] This definition derives from the psychoanalytic theory pioneered by Sigmund Freud in the early part of the 20th century. To Freud and others, "the human personality" is a distinctive identity belonging to everyone. Fine, but the root word for personality is Latin *persona*, which means mask and a mask is a cover-up. If the ego's work is to respond to the immediate, surrounding world, then what could it cover up other than the opposite—the eternal, infinite universe. Therefore, our personality covers up something essential to our being. The ego is not the essential self; rather, it is something temporary—a transient construct that creates the mask, which covers up who we really are.

We usually think that the personality comprises only the intellectual, emotional, and moral aspects of our life. The mask consists of much more than these three *mental* aspects; it must also include the four *physical* assets with which we meet life—our body, our talents, our intelligences[20], and our temperament[21]. The latter three aspects have profound influences on the first three, and all six qualities belong to our genes. In other words, they comprise our *form*.

All six come under pressure from the environment, with intellect, emotion, and morality being more sensitive to those pressures, and form, temperament, and talent more resistant to them. The ego's job is to create an individual. It works with these assets. The finite ego focuses on that life which exists between birth and death—between dust and ashes. This makes it secular, and, if it is not made aware of the spiritual resources that stand behind it, it perceives that it must develop itself out of these genetic attributes. If life only begins in dust and ends in ashes, this can become a lonely struggle.

There can be no doubt that the ego is extremely valuable. Sigmund Freud recognized the value of the ego[22] for each person, and I believe that he looked at the ego as the navigator of the ship of life—I certainly do. He also saw it responding to our genetically driven, instinctual self—what he called the id—and to the tempering controls of family and social traditions—the superego. It may help to look at these three aspects of self in terms of human development: the id is ancient history, the ego is modern history, and the superego is postmodern history.

We could not have reached these proportions of ego-based function without simple beginnings, beginnings lost in our pre-recorded history. Our egos have responded to stress for a long time, and each one of us follows the course of human history in our own ego development—we wrote the program.

Where does the ego live?

Humans everywhere appreciate that each one of us has a force or energy within that keeps us alive. This life force gathers in seven specific centers of the body called, in Sanskrit, chakras (wheels). They line up in front of the spine from your tailbone to the top of your skull. Each one has its own power and needs. The first chakra lies in the perineal body where your legs join; it relates to those activities and needs that sustain life. The second, found just below your navel in the pit of the stomach, relates to the energy of physical creativity: our children, our jobs, and our income. The third lies in the solar plexus—the sun center—the center of control and the home of the ego, the mistress of control. The fourth is the heart center, the energy of love and seat of the soul. The fifth is in the throat and is the center of communication and surrender to a Higher Will with its integrating power of truth and honesty. The sixth lies behind "the third eye" in the center of the forehead.... It is the creative energy of thought and discernment. The seventh is in the crown of the head.... It is the home of our spiritual connection and its energy.

The ego has its home in our energy system; one perfectly suited to its need for control. From its point of view, it tends to focus its energies downward, nurturing our needs of the physical body: food, clothing, shelter, family and tribal protection, procreation, and gainful service. In short, it focuses on its physical world, just as science focuses on the physical universe. We use the vast riches of our minds by reaching up in service of our bodies to Spirit circumventing the homes of the soul and the higher Will as if they were not there. By ignoring chakras, 4, 5, and 6—Love, Truth, and Honesty—we have left out the filter that keeps us from misapplying knowledge, and have relied entirely on the ego for those functions. Thus we have created the source of all of our harmful behaviors.

How does the ego develop?

The ego must figure out how to use our physical assets to shape our personalities and survive. Ego development begins in earnest at about the age of five after we have developed our physical and emotional senses and peaks some twenty years later. Its strength continues, unabated, for about the next ten years. At this point, it begins to weaken and if it is not aware of its spiritual counterpart, the soul, it usually calls forth a final burst of ego energy in the so-called *midlife crisis*—a literal and figurative "Battle of the Bulge".

Ego development begins in our childhood homes, continues in our schools, and moves on into our workplaces, adult homes, and families. You can understand that, with but rare exception, our ego's encounters—its experiences—shape our personalities. These encounters often take the form of a contest that always ends with one party winning and the other losing. Survival is indeed the ego's game.

Individuation

Fortunately—and with rare exceptions—none of us grow up alone. To do so is almost impossible and always highly dangerous, for there is no history and its lessons. As George Santayana reminds us, "Those who cannot remember the past are condemned to repeat it," and we learn about the past from other people. Ironically, although we need each other, independence from each other is essential. Indeed, the growing child's first pronoun is always "me," as in, "Me do it!" From our earliest beginnings, the ego, our judging, differentiating function, learns the difference between "me" and "you." It then gathers and repeats the experience of differentiating between self and others, what psychologists call individuation. The more it knows about itself, the more navigational skill it acquires.

Individuation is the goal of a healthy personality that naturally and comfortably brings together ego and higher parts of self.

This process results in the maturation of that human quality which relates to others, to nature, and to spirit—the soul. Through it, each one of us becomes a unique person, a one-of-a-kind work of art.

Individuation applies to all personalities. It inheres in all human beings with the ability to work for the entire lifetime of every individual. It is a learning process that has no limit. The degree to which it succeeds depends on inherited strengths and the quality and quantity of nurturance in the environment in which the individual develops, especially in those vital first five years that develop all the senses that we use to evaluate the environment. For the sake of our world, we must continuously apply the maxim: "It takes a community to raise a child."

Individuation even applies to and separates identical twins—clones of each other. Usually within thirty-six hours of their birth, their mothers can tell them apart by their cries! Their temperaments and talents are identical, but they become individuals. As they grow, their families and close friends can always distinguish them, even if only by subtle differences.

Cloning may happen by chance, as well. We have a finite number of genes with which to make a human being (estimates range from 30,000 to 100,000[23]), so we are limited to having only a few billion ways of making humans. Your clone could be alive today! If you two were to meet and spend some time together, you would find that not only do you look alike, but also you have similarities of temperament and talents. Beyond that, however, you would meet the divergent effects of growing up in different environments. You would have different life experiences and knowledge, although you would have virtually identical ways of responding to them. Though we can clone bodies in this dynamic, constantly changing world and its universe, we cannot clone knowledge and experience. They are individual, unique to each one of us. We can safely say that no two of us are alike.

These conditions of diversity and dissimilarity encourage separation and nurture isolation. The Western World does little to nurture connectedness, so the ego comes to believe that it is the only navigator of the ship of life. Even if it does acknowledge the existence of a "Higher Power" in the creation of all people, places and things, it believes that only it matters. With its power of judging, it has made hard choices of effective behaviors and attitudes, cutting out the ones that do not work, and condemning them to secret, shadowy cells.

The ego keeps an inventory of that which it has condemned to these shadows, framing all in the judging attitude of fear. Fear creates attachments to the past and colors them with the stepchildren of fear: blame, guilt, and shame. The first two demand that we see our thoughts and resulting actions as mistakes that we should have been able to correct from the outset. The third says that we are the mistake and that we cannot do better—the legacy of the Garden of Eden.

The ability to sort things out and tell them apart without attachments to the past is the higher-order function of discernment. The ability to discern brings wisdom into the situation. Indeed, a wise person is seen as a discerning person. We usually perceive wisdom as a property of aging and maturity. When the brash youth evolves into the statesman, his ego lets go of its stranglehold on the past and any hope of changing it and he now practices discernment. He has forgiven himself of his past, for the essential meaning of forgive is to give away—to let go!

By the time ego has finished shaping the self, what originally looked to it as a glistening sphere of human energy has acquired pits, gouges, and dull, opaque areas in its clear, deep, shining surface. None of these wounds looks good to the judge. However, ego knows it is strong and functional in the broken places, regardless of its appearance. After all, it developed those functions to help it navigate life. It is proof of its own success... just ask it! And that hubris lies behind all the trouble we find ourselves in to this day!

Following the law of attraction—like-seeks-like—the ego will seek out others with whom it shares similar qualities of temperament and talents. It does so for the simple reason that it gets positive, nurturing strokes from the group, be it a religious congregation, a service club, a social club, or the Ku Klux Klan. Nurturing is essential for life and growth; without it, we wither and die.

In 1937, not yet four years old, I received a wound that set the direction of my life. I tried to dig clams with a garden rake at high tide, a hundred yards from the clam flat where I used to visit with the clam diggers. I was so stubborn in my quest for the clams that the water soon got over my head—I could better see what my rake brought up! According to my mother, I would have drowned had her sister not seen me disappear under water and dashed into the bay, ruining her best summer dress in order to rescue me[24].

When she got me up in the air, had spun me around to see if I was still breathing, and had given me a good shake to get my attention, she hollered, "Toby, you stupid little boy!" She did not know that her fearfully violent grab had terrified me beyond belief and my soul had dissociated before the lift, shake, and spin, leaving my ego to find out how stupid it was. Thus we set the stage for my life's work—stopping abuse and helping people discover their unique gifts.

Needless to say, my ego withdrew from my aunt. It also withdrew from my mother to whom Aunt Brunie carried me, stuffed under her arm like a sack of flour. It wrote out a set of rules of safe behavior that would protect me from everybody who might hurt me: Rule one, withdraw from people, and row your own boat, it's safer; Rule two, be judgmental, it will protect you; and Rule three, dissociate when another person's anger gets unbearable. In addition, it created a safe little world of reading, studying, and learning that included adults with whom I could discuss things. I had few friends my age and I resisted my mother's pressures to "make friends." Mother thrived on "making friends," but my life rules said that closeness to others was not safe because I might get hurt; after all, her sister and she should have been my friends, right?

The judgment my aunt handed me then stuck with me for fifty years! By now, my ego considers itself an expert in deciding what comprises a "stupid" behavior. Furthermore, it is also an expert at fixing stupid behaviors, and that could easily relate to my choice of a medical career. It could also relate to my ready anger at a telephone call that got me out of bed to fix a drunk hurt in an accident of his or her own making.

Surgery may fix physical trauma caused by stupid behaviors, but it does not fix the behaviors. I tried correcting stupidity in other ways and, as I look back, I see that all my attempts to fix such behavior came from my need to heal my own wound! However, in attempting to fix others, I sometimes hurt them. Fortunately for everyone, as my healing progressed, my hurtful ways diminished.

Ego remembers. It keeps inventories, and uses them for its own selfish purposes. Ego always works to correct the painful happenings of its early experience because it wants to feel better. In its own way, it creates defenses against the old trauma. With its ability to remember, it tries to make each new situation fit into its experience so that it can defend itself according to what worked once before. It awakens its judgment and looks for someone to make guilty of the mistake, and subject to the simplest accusation "stupid".

My experience tells me that we must stop accusing people of being stupid. Of course, this relates to my childhood experience…and I am not alone. It saddens me to consider how many people have been accused of being "stupid" in their developing years. When I tell any group of people my experience of being called "stupid" (p. 35), I ask how many of them have been called "stupid" and a forest of hands springs up. Calling a person "stupid" does not make anyone intelligent.

Dissing

Tragically, we still believe in the power of this dismissing word to make good, intelligent people out of our children. It does not work. Insulting others, especially children, never works; it marginalizes them. This puts them at the fringe of the society to which they desperately want to belong. Naturally, that part of them that is concerned with survival leads them to create a new society of similarly marginalized people who can support each other's egos. They will create a name like "Skinheads" and revert to ancient tribal behaviors that justify harming others… in exactly the same way that they were harmed.

Today's high school students are acutely aware of the harmfulness of disrespect and dismissal, which they call "dissing." In some juvenile societies, when a person is "dissed," s/he is considered justified in taking extreme measures, up to and including murder. As horrible as that may be, it reflects the opinion of a important segment of society that dissing is a totally unacceptable behavior. Someday we shall never again use that "s——d" word.

The more we find it unacceptable to subject another person to dismissal or disrespect, the more we must direct ourselves to find another, more acceptable, behavior, lest the old one return, for nature abhors all vacuums. We must realize that everyone tries his or her best to learn how to get along with others. We all need encouragement rather than dismissal. We have to take the "dis-" out of "disrespect," and the respect we develop for each other will reach beyond the fear and attack of the old behavior to the love and compassion of the new. Ego finds this hard work, but help can come from many sources.

How the ego works:

The "survival response" and the ego:

This is the "fight-or-flight" survival response that I talked about in the Prologue (p. 4). It took many thousands of years to write the genetic code for this, and our genes renewed it, generation after generation for the few times a year we needed it to help us handle a life-threatening situation.

We still need this survival response, but because of our high speed, high stress life, we use it every day, often several times a day, and often inappropriately. Because of its reflexive, life-saving nature, our survival response is set up to fire off after only a superficial evaluation of the life-threat of any given situation. However, the cumulative effects of a series of apparently innocuous, only mildly stressful, events can trigger it. Once activated, the response goes on afterburners; after all, its purpose is to save the threatened life. These powerful effects on our bodies and minds can last for as long as forty-eight hours after the incident is past.

The code in our genes tells our bodies to respond to life threats with two powerful chemicals: adrenaline and cortisol. They are intended for short-term use only because adrenaline increases heart rate and blood pressure; and cortisol raises blood sugar levels and suppresses the immune system. These reactions are essential to fighting or fleeing. However, the long-term effects of these chemicals are hypertension, heart attacks, adult onset diabetes, cancer, and most of the disorders of the immune system. That which saved our lives in our past has become a major threat to our lives in the present.

You can see that this helpful survival response has its dark side: Repeated small stresses of the barking dog kind can build up to levels that elicit the same response as a roaming, hungry lion. When the stresses build up like this, the possibility of preventing violence gets all too slim.

Our problems with the survival response grow first out of the ego's undying commitment to survival and second out of today's social environment replacing yesterday's natural environment. Humans rather than predatory animals have become the trigger of the survival response.

The ego uses memory and judgment to keep an inventory of everything it feels ever harmed it. It adds up all the insults of the day and carries the inventory everywhere it goes, becoming progressively ready to defend itself against further insult. In the aggressive environment of a highway crowded with others in the same state of mind, the blat of a horn can trigger the murderous response we call "road rage" . Should the trigger not appear on the way home, it can appear in the behavior of an excited, shouting child; or an harassed spouse can say just the wrong word, and all hell breaks loose. The object has just become a hungry tiger!

The survival response is a time bomb that goes off without any respect for who is near it. To defuse the ticking bomb in our brains, we often sedate ourselves with addictive behaviors, which can add to the response when our drug of choice is no longer available. No, defusing the bomb can only be done with love.

Memory and judgment

That traumatic clam-digging incident from my childhood (p.35) demonstrates how the ego uses its experience to help it respond to new circumstances. Subsequent to this episode, I had a terrible fear of water that my mother attributed to the near drowning. For years, whenever she brought it up, I could remember being underwater, completely happy and busily raking up round gray rocks that looked like clams. Try as I might, however, I had no memory of the rescue by my aunt. I could only remember looking up and seeing silvery ripples in the surface of the water over my head, and in that moment I was at perfect peace.

Fifty years later, in a workshop on healing the "inner child," by recovering repressed childhood memories, I remembered. Under the gentle direction of the workshop leader, a gifted, shamanic psychologist from New Zealand, David Groves, Ph.D., I remembered my aunt grabbing me from behind, jerking me out of the water, spinning me around, and screaming at me for being a stupid little boy! In the fifty years between that dramatic episode and meeting Groves, my life had a distinct, consistent, repetitive, and powerfully judgmental focus on "stupid" behavior and the person who committed it, especially if I was that person.

Moreover, every few years, I would find myself moving inexorably into a situation in which I *knew* I was going to make a serious and "stupid" mistake. When it happened, someone got incredibly angry with me for my stupidity. When that person's anger struck me, I would become speechless, feel helpless, and tremble inside—I would *dissociate* while that person had her or his verbal way with me. This feeling was horrible, so horrible that I have no other way of describing it even today.

When that person left my presence, puzzled by my silence and looking at me strangely (probably reflecting the strange look in my eyes), I would viciously berate myself for being stupid. I knew I could control my anger, but I could not control these strange behaviors that had, as I look back, so much to do with both stupidity and anger. I wanted very much to resolve this weird behavior and the Universe provided me with the solution at David Groves' workshop where I remembered the first time anyone called me "stupid.".

When I had gone through the trauma (in my memories) and survived it, the dysfunctional behavior ended! Now, no longer stupid, I became a defender of those who would suffer emotional abuse from being called "stupid." Even later, I would champion people of all intellectual ranges, even those whom others might call "stupid."

Once I re-experienced the original emotional trauma, I understood—my ego, good old fellow, had set about to protect me from ever getting hurt in this way again. It had developed a set of rules of safe behavior based entirely on its perceptions of that clam-digging incident (p. 35). My ego had tried always to make those rules work for every threatening situation, but not all threatening situations were like my terrified and terrifying aunt accusing me of being "stupid."

You can imagine what happened when my ego tried to make every threatening situation look like one in which I had done something stupid. Confusing, is it not? When I recovered that memory in 1987, I could see how and when my ego jumped into uncomfortable situations to look for the "stupid" person who caused it. It helped me become aware of the damaging effects of thinking that people are "stupid" when, in reality, they are trying their best to work through a problem. To counter my old tendencies, I have developed gentle practices of encouraging myself to look at the situation through compassionate eyes, and let go of the need to judge it. My daily mantram is, therefore, "Today we are all doing our best; tomorrow we shall do better." It is a work in progress, and its challenges are likely to continue for the rest of my life.

I believe that recovering that memory in 1987 would not have been possible had my ego not started on that healing path in 1975. At that time, my life was full of stress and I was not dealing with it at all well. When my practice manager loaned me Earl Nightingale's tape in which Earl suggested that the anger around me was a reflection of my own anger, I went through a purely intellectual process of deciding that I would change the anger. I could have started with the feeling, but I was a thinking person to the exclusion of virtually all feeling. Yes, I was even numb to my own anger! I had been using it to control circumstances for the better part of my life and I could not imagine how I could change it. I could intellectually see that anger was counterproductive and that I needed to let it go. Somehow, I felt awkward and embarrassed—nervous—when I thought of changing it. Little wonder, though, for this is my ego setting rules based on its past experience.

Over the ensuing years, it became clear to me that the ego is an essential part of every human being, even though you and I might not like the way it works. The navigator-ego stays actively involved in life in order to hear from the environment how it is doing just as the navigator of any ship needs to keep an eye on the radar screens and out the cabin windows. The ego needs to judge itself and its performance, too. It bases its actions on its past so it seeks out familiar judging environments because it knows how to respond to them. The need to judge grows out of fear, and this, in turn, causes the ego to choose either defensive or aggressive behaviors (both of which are angry) in order to control the situation. How often have you heard the expression, "the best defense is a good offense"? (In other words, "Control this with your anger.)

How does the ego get us in trouble?

In four ways:

Misperceptions

Separation

Projecting in time and space

Judgment

The ego's awareness of life is tragically, desperately finite.... It is destined to begin in dust and end in ashes. Once the ego learns to take the measure of the world with its physical and emotional senses, it sets up a courtroom in the mind to cope with every life situation it meets. It plays every role in the courtroom from police detective to judge. It even plays the role of the accused!

That unfortunate role predominates in the lives of many, revealing itself in the expression, "how could I be so stupid?" Have *you* ever called yourself "stupid"? Have you ever asked, "How could I be so stupid?" These horribly ugly put-downs accuse you of having made a mistake and you should have known better. Guilty! Punishment follows... from the person making the accusation. How often is that person you?

With enough of these judgments, you will become the mistake! In that tragic state, you cannot know better. You are now sentenced and committed to a life of punishment for your sin of stupidity. Take a moment to review for yourself how this plays out in your own life. Think of others similarly punished. Consider the behaviors that we adopt to try to compensate for these sins! Look around you; they are everywhere!

All of this is the work of the ego. Its punishment is relentless and severe. The sentence is death!

If you recoil from this, remember what we believe happened in the Garden of Eden. God shunned us for our shameful sin of acquiring knowledge.[25] He made us feel shame. When we shame ourselves, we shun ourselves. We act out of our shame and our belief that others are trying to shame us. The result is murder. The wars of the last century murdered 100 million people. This is the measure of our shame... and it makes no sense.

In this ego-created scenario, judgment, based on the past, creates punishing attack in the present. In the present, the ego maintains an image of an equally punishing, fearful future. All of these ego functions arise from misperceptions of the truth... the simple truth that tells us there are no mistakes, only lessons. Life is a learning experience remarkably similar to that of learning to walk—you have to fall down, and you get up again, and again, and again, in spite of the bloody nose.

Healing the ego's mistakes:

Superego

We have spent the better part of one hundred years recognizing and defining our ego, as defined by Sigmund Freud. Today, we are seriously trying to define the "self," part of which is the ego. Another "part of self," the superego, comes out of our recognition of our ego's potential for destructive, rapacious behavior. It comprises the social customs, ethics, and mores that we use to govern each other. It is a group of egos working together with collective memories to find those patterns of social behavior that work better than others do. The judging, perceiving egos that create a superego can also subject its truth to terrible distortions in exactly the same way that an individual ego can distort individual truth. You can easily find examples of this throughout history, some of the most monstrous examples of which took place in the century that just ended.

We use the superego to control harmful behaviors in socially approved ways. When we choose a destructive force to limit the ego's destructive power, we challenge the ego in its home territory, and stack the results in favor of the ego. We shall have to choose another way over which fear and aggression do not rule. That way is love.

We shall have to learn to love our ego. With the ego's ability to do harm where it feels fear, loving the ego seems risky. The ego's ability to come together with other egos and create the superego reduces this risk. The superego, always reflecting society's wishes, continually seeks the better way, and creates safe environments like support groups for such loving meetings. A superego works because the egos that comprise it choose to be in relationship with each other. Thus we formed the first extended family—the earliest tribe. It has developed ever-higher standards of relationship, attaining such levels today as the United Nations, the World Council of Churches, and the World Court.

Loving the ego

Some spiritual practices disparage the ego by describing it as fearful, judgmental, guilt-ridden, and subject to repeated misperceptions of reality. In doing so, they judge the judge. I disagree with such practices because of my own terrifying experience of attack, terror, shame, and guilt. I see value in my ego—and in the egos of others. Ego has valuable qualities, even though it has limited perceptions.[26]

Our attitudes have a significant effect on how we perceive things. Attitudes color, shape, and frame how we perceive, and they work together in a great variety of ways. The two most powerful attitudes are love and fear. They are the basis for all the others such as anger, grief, envy, joy, and happiness. Even though our perceptions are limited, we navigate quite well with them. However, we must make room for improvement… and believe that we can improve.

The ego, devoted to its own survival, naturally does its best with whatever resources it has. It continually reacts to what it perceives to be the actions of "the surrounding physical and social world." The ego is our worldly navigator, wily and resourceful in its ability to respond to these actions. It is our secular guide in the secular world.

In order to develop its navigational skills, the ego must first come to know itself as an individual. To do this, it must use its senses—its physical feelings—to become aware of the presence of a whole flotilla of ships around it, steered by navigators of widely varying degrees of experience, knowledge, and self-awareness. It has to take the helm of its ship, trim sail, and set out on course— alone—avoiding collisions with the other ships of the flotilla. Separation is the way of the ego, believing it has to figure life out by and for itself. To help it separate from the others, it uses attitudes—its feelings. Remember, the ego "evaluates, plans, and in other ways is responsive to and acts in the surrounding physical and social world (p. 29)." The ego believes it is the only one sailing the ship, so it has to teach itself how to trim sail, set course, and avoid collisions.

Something compels us to stand and walk... it compels us to learn. It sends us on quests of all kinds... and sometimes we do not return. There is something more to us than just our egos; so look at yourself with kind and loving eyes. Put out of your mind the unjust courtroom with its judge on a high place above everyone else. Come now to the open circle of spiritual counselors who will help you learn your lessons.

Even though the word, ego, can be used as an acronym for "easing god out,"[27] we may do well to consider that God had something to do with the creation of the ego. If It didn't, then the ego is an accident. The Grand Expansion of creation is not an accident. Our DNA is no accident. The genetically determined attributes of the personality are no accidents. That finite part of self that uses the qualities of personality to navigate the ocean of life cannot be an accident; it can only be a product of Divine Intention, and the ego deserves to be held in that divine light. Perhaps then, easing God out is only an incidence of the misapplication of knowledge and, when all is said and done, we shall discover that developing and concentrating ego strengths are God-seeking behaviors. Consider, then, that the ego is that part of self which *seeks* God.

When we come to look at the ego this way, we can use our soft eyes of compassion to acknowledge that everybody is doing her or his best in view of the circumstances of their life. As I said earlier (p. 33), the ultimate success of the process of life depends not only on genes, but also on the quality and quantity of nurturing given the person during her or his formative, childhood years. This process determines the quality and quantity of nurturing the person will give throughout her or his life, for what we sow in our early years becomes what we reap in our later years.

Acknowledging that survival is always in the ego's best interests, and that the projective nature of fear and anger have been an essential part of its methods of survival, we would do well by looking at the dark side of these two feelings—the harm that comes from them. Harm returns harm, and we are beginning to discover how damaging that can be. We can spare our selves a lot of grief by learning to red-flag every impending action that could harm self or others. When the ego is about to make a crucial decision, recalling this directive helps keep us *out of harm's way*[28].

It helps to remember that harm never comes from hope and love, only from fear and anger, the ego's attitudes that created separation. The more we succeed in staying free of harm, the more we are in a position to benefit others. When we choose to let go of fear, we move out of separation into relationship; we share our lives with others. Fear's defensive, fight-or-flight survival-based attitudes fade now, replaced by the empowering, creative embrace of love. Love comes to us from a different part of self—the soul— the captain of our ship. Let us go to the captain's quarters and the life that changes our focus from surviving to thriving.

Chapter 3: Soul, the Captain of the Ship of Life— Immersed in Life.

You would not find out the boundaries of soul, even by traveling along every path: so deep a measure does it have.

–Heraclitus

Souls of people, on their way to Earth-life, pass through a room full of lights; each takes a taper, often only a spark, to guide it in the dim country of this world. But some souls, by rare fortune, are detained longer and have time to grasp a handful of tapers, which they weave into a torch. These are the torch-bearers of humanity, its poets, seers, and saints, who lead and lift the race out of darkness, toward the light. They are the law-givers and saviors, the light-bringers, way-showers and truth-tellers, and without them, humanity would lose its way in the dark.

—Plato

Somewhere deep within you is a song that plays softly, always...
A song you can hear only if you're very quiet, and very still
A song of life, and dreams, and wisdom
A call to adventure on a path that is uniquely yours.
Take time to listen to the song of your soul
And see where it leads you.

—Author unknown

"We all come to earth with field orders."

—Søren Kierkegaard

(Soul) is the indirect presence of your spirit and in your soul sleep all the possibilities of your human destiny.

—John O'Donohue

Principles:

- The Soul comes here *on* our DNA to give the personality a passion with which to approach life.
- The Soul comes here to use the individual's ego strengths to create an adventure of universal experience.
- The soul's spiritual balance leads the ego through harm's way into God's way.

Important first considerations:

Consider that some 2500 years elapsed between the time of Heraclitus and the time of John O'Donohue. Though the words are different, the thoughts and the feelings they elicit are similar. A richness of joy and peace pervades them, and fear and anger—the basis of all harm—fade away into illusion. You may wonder, quite appropriately, that if these qualities of the soul have been with us for two and one-half millennia, why is it that we continue to inflict so much harm on each other? Part of the answer lies in our need to develop the ego to the point where we come to realize that we cannot continue to live any longer under its sole direction. Part of the answer lies in our need to understand the soul and its ability to be passionately present to the suffering caused by the separated ego. The rest of the answer lies in the accumulated suffering we have perpetrated on each other for the last 7,500 years. Friends, we must work to heal those wounds of the past.[29]

Consider that all harm to the body and mind comes from a starvation in the human ego—a spiritual starvation. This, the greatest of all hungers, has a terrible, fearful effect on the ego, for this arises from the greatest loneliness of all—that of parental abandonment. Remember, oh children of Abraham, that the legendary Formative Principle, whom Abraham called God, and whom Jesus called Abba, reputedly threw us out of His house and home for our sin of eating the fruit that taught us about both good and evil. Children, our ego must compensate for the hunger—it ravens for its Source.

Consider that this great hunger underlies all abuse of weaker beings, all road rage, all domestic violence, and all terrorism. Consider that it lies behind all addictive, escape behaviors. Add others to this list from your experience. Are we not all well aware of the effects of that ravenous behavior which seems to have been with us since the beginning of time? Would you like to satisfy that hunger without devouring others? Call, then, on that part of self that knows its divine Source—your soul.

If you are wondering how you can call on your soul, you have a lot of company, for we are not used to that communication. Our society does not consciously nurture the soul's presence in its children; so, early on in life, the ego develops a belief in its power to live life by its self and stops listening to the song of the soul. However, you can listen—once again.

Do you remember your mother's answer when you asked her that profoundly existential question, "Mummy, who am I and where did I come from?"

My mother said, "My dear, you're Toby, and you came from mummy's tummy." I had finally asked a question that she could not refer to my father for an answer (p. 21).

However, that brought the conversation to an abrupt end! She probably wondered, "What in heaven's name ever led my child to ask such a question?"

I was not looking for that answer; I wanted to know who I really was, and what kind of a place I had come from to be in her tummy! I was losing a memory and wanted to hold onto it like the little girl who wanted her newborn brother to tell her about God (p.8). She had probably already asked her mother the question of her origin and had gotten the "mummy's tummy" answer. She was looking for a transpersonal answer to that question—a soul answer—not an anatomical answer... and she knew her baby brother had it!

As the ego is all about *what* a person is; the soul is all about *who*[30] a person is. The "who" of our existence derives from the spiritual Mystery of the source of all life… we have all been here since the beginning of time. The subatomic particles that make up our bodies all came into being in the first fraction of a second of the life of the universe. As we were there then, so we are here now; promised this life from the beginning of time by the Source of life, Itself. The Source has called us to life, so every life is a gift. The source could never make a mistake (or else we would not be here). It has blessed us with life. Life will wound us, and our wounds will determine the nature of our ultimate gift back to Life. Our egos will see our wounds as curses…. Our souls will put the wounds "back under the blessing (Nouwen)" and transform them into our individual gift to Life. This is *who* we are.

What is the soul?

In H.O.P.E. Groups and SoulCircling workshops, where we help people establish a dialogue with their soul, people often ask me what soul is and if it isn't the same as their spirit. Have you ever wondered what soul means? Let us see what kind of answers might be available.

The Encyclopædia Britannica has this to say about soul:
> "in religion and philosophy, (soul is) the immaterial aspect or essence of a human being, that which confers individuality and humanity, often considered to be synonymous with the mind or the self. In theology, the soul is further defined as that part of the individual which partakes of divinity and often is considered to survive the death of the body[31]."

As I examine the words of the writer from The Encyclopædia Britannica, I find five aspects of the soul to which I would like to draw your attention:

1. The soul is the "immaterial essence of a human being." The soul is not material—not of the body—and yet its presence is vital to our being, our essence.

2. The soul "confers individuality and humanity." That must mean that the soul is essential to our humanness—

that which we all share—and at the same time, it is a part of our remarkable, extensive, and unrepeated differences. Today about seven billion human beings live on the face of the earth, and as no two of us are exactly physically alike (even identical twins) no two of us are exactly psycho-spiritually alike. As there is a different body for each one of us, so there is a different soul for each one of us.

3. The soul is "considered to be synonymous with the mind or the self." This creates an identity between mind and self. The Self is our individuality—those unique qualities that distinguish one person from another and that comprise both ego and soul. Mind, our collection of conscious and unconscious processes that influence behaviors of all kinds, becomes transpersonal thereby— greater than the brain. Indeed, the late 18th century British poet and artist, William Blake, is credited with saying, "My brain is an organ my mind finds useful." In this way, the soul becomes that precious quality and quantity of personal and transpersonal knowledge and experience which is unique in and to every one of us.

4. The soul is "that part of an individual which partakes of divinity." It *knows* Truth—that which cannot be interpreted—and God, the source of Truth.

5. The soul is commonly "considered to survive the death of the body." It has eternal aspects—it precedes me and succeeds me.

My finite "Ken Hamilton" existence first said "me" when I was about two, and so did yours. At about that time I met a dream companion who told me his name was "Rookie," the "oo" of which he pronounced like the "oo" of "booty" rather than "cookie." He was so real that I played with him in my waking hours as much as I did in my dreaming time. He was older than I was and knew a lot more about life. He was wise—as if he had already lived a long,

long time. What he taught me then guides me still. He continues to guide me today. He is my infinite, Rookie, existence with such an appropriate name. When you were small, did you have such a companion, an "imaginary childhood playmate"? Where did s/he come from, and where is s/he now?

Soul and spirit:

We commonly make the mistake of using soul and spirit synonymously. We are confused about their meaning. It has not always been so. Prior to the scientific revolution and the Age of Reason (p. 9), people in western societies believed that their being had four parts: body, mind, soul, and spirit. The Age of Reason maintained that we were no more than a linked body and mind[32] because Reason could not measure and define either soul or spirit and it believed that they did not exist. It would have discarded them both were it not for the Vatican's tight hold on spirit. We came close to losing Soul in this confusing shuffle, but, clever lady that she is, she camouflaged herself by becoming (almost) synonymous with spirit. There, with time on her side, she waited until the time was right for her to reveal herself—again.

In order for us to correct our confusion, it helps to go back to the Occidental origins of the concepts of soul and spirit—ancient Greece and Rome. The ancient Greeks believed that the goddess, Psyche, whose name also means butterfly, was the symbol of the embodied soul. Psyche was a human woman who had fallen in love with Apollo and who succeeded in doing something very few humans do: she looked into his face in the light of day, which made him fall in love with her... and he was already betrothed to the goddess, Aphrodite! It was only after Psyche had admitted to Aphrodite how she had seduced Apollo and subsequently submitted to Aphrodite's wrathful punishment that Zeus made Psyche a goddess, too. Psyche is certainly full of love and passion; she is intimate, personal, and feminine. The ancient Romans' Latin word for soul is *anima* (a *feminine* noun), the feminine principle of life.

On the other hand, the Greeks believed that the breath, *pneuma*, was the symbol of the disembodied spirit; after all, they could not see or measure either the spirit or the breath; yet they knew that, like the breath, spirit was essential to life. The ancient Romans shared this belief with the Greeks, and their masculine word for the breath, *spiritus*, is the origin of our word, spirit.

The breath is as immaterial and intangible as the air of which it is made. On a frosty morning, should you live in the colder climes, breathe out and watch your breath as you do. It makes a small cloud that lasts but a moment before dissipating into the surrounding air, no longer identifiable with its source—you. If you live in a warmer climate, breathe onto a chilled mirror and watch the moisture become a film that rapidly evaporates. In much the same way that we cannot see the breath without help, our senses cannot perceive the spirit without help. Spirit is not individually human, but common to everything. It is universal, impersonal, and masculine. Our senses cannot perceive the presence of spirit the way they can perceive the presence of soul. Soul does not dissipate into an invisible something after you have caught a glimpse of it; it remains recognizable and identifiable, subtle and tangible. The soul is the chill in the air or the cool mirror that makes it possible to see evidence of the intangible spirit.

A little bit of background:

Our souls have been a part of us for a long time, as you can see from Plato's words above. However, as I said earlier (p. 9), when The Enlightenment, the age of reason, arose out of the scientific revolution of the 16th century, the Occidental world became convinced that reason and logic were the only way to the Truth. We threw out thoughts and things for which we could find no objective, reasoned evidence to validate their existence. Soul failed the test of objective reason and we left it by the wayside.

However, René Descartes, the father of modern rationalism, whose thoughts on the body and mind are fundamental to contemporary Western philosophy of science, concluded that the soul and the mind were the same. He took it from its home in the heart, and stuck it in the brain. And we have been living soul-less, ego-driven lives ever since. By making soul a mind function, he preserved it for its (re-) discovery late in the last century. Poor ego, for three hundred years, it has been trying to do it all alone from its residence in the solar plexus[33], hungering for its home in The Source and not knowing that its guide to that source dwells in the heart immediately above it.

The soul could never stay in the recesses of the brain; it is the life force that keeps us alive. Even Hitler had to have a fragment of soul hidden deep in the recesses of his incredibly evil, ego-directed being. It only left when his ego condemned his body and fatally damaged it.

The soul has the patience that kept Job alive through all his suffering. It has waited in that patience until the time came for its re-emergence from reason's intellectual abandonment of it. That same spiritual patience enables it to encompass compassionately the being of a murderer, a rapist, or a terrorist. Because of the ever-expanding, widespread, murderous events of the past two hundred years, we are at the bottom of a deep pool of suffering. The soul's eternal patience will be rewarded... evil is ephemeral.

John O'Donohue[34] tells us that soul comes here to love and be loved. *A Course in Miracles*[35] tells us that we can always perceive others as extending love or giving a call for help. Neither statement explains why some souls come to inhabit bodies directed by evil egos—egos that define love in their own narcissistically self-satisfying, corrupt, destructive ways. These beings collect their energy from the human experience of "fight-or-flight" responses to fearful situations and the ego's use of fear to control and dominate others (p. 4). They come to teach us to love one another, to love God, and to know that evil must ultimately bow in surrender to love. These lessons are extremely difficult to learn, for they keep coming back, seemingly without much in the way of quantitative or qualitative differences. They have done so for several thousand years.

Crisis:

However, I think that we are finally "getting it." We are learning to recognize the presence of a huge hole in our sidewalk[36], into which we have fallen so many times and have always blamed somebody or something else (usually some form of God) for our misfortune. As long as we deny the existence of soul, the shaping of the young human takes place without much regard for our spiritual nature. Our soul, intimately connected to that divine form, blames neither the Creator nor the ego for the fall; for it knows that in our painful crashes lie lessons that show us the Truth. In this time in human history, soul returns to our awareness as a guide to the truth.

As long as an ego believes that it did not make that hole and that it can get out of it all by itself, it will fall back into it and continue to blame somebody or something else for its misfortune. When it decides to surrender and take responsibility for what happens, it will see the soul standing at the edge of the hole, ready to throw a safety harness tied to a climbing rope wrapped around its waist. Now, when the ego gets out of the hole, it is ready to engage in dialog with its friendly helper.

Falling in the hole—crisis—gives us the greatest opportunity for this dialog. Crises assume a plethora of forms with profound effects on everyone...little wonder that the Chinese ideogram for crisis is the symbol for opportunity on top of the symbol for danger. Crisis is always an opportunity to listen to Spirit speak through your soul. Your soul, knowing you so well, chooses the best way to get you to listen. Sometimes, and always as a last resort, it has to choose your body. My patients often showed me how they had come to realize that their diseases were expressions of chronic, previously unaddressed, or denied life-crises. In other words, their diseases were actually symptoms of much more profound psychospiritual conditions.

My patients taught me so much that was not taught in medical school in 1960. One striking exception came from a clinical instructor who said to my eight-student group, "When you have finished taking a history and finding the "what," "where," "when," and "how" of the symptoms, you might just want to ask, 'Why?' You could be in for a big surprise."

Today, with the pressures of technologies and time constraints in healthcare delivery, there is little time for even that question in the practice of medicine[37]. However, I enjoin my fellow practitioners of medicine and surgery to consider that there are moments in which that question may be the single most important thing that they can ask their patient or themselves.[38] When "I wonder why," seems to whisper softly in the background, it is really a scream. When physicians hear that whisper and ask the question, it usually opens a floodgate. "Oh God," they cry, "there goes managed care—again." The secret to therapeutic success in these cases is letting go of all need to try to fix this new situation and to simply sit and listen—the healing has begun—the patient's inner therapist has just announced its presence. Meet the soul. Virtually every practitioner of medicine has had such opportunities to open her or his awareness to the presence of soul. This process may well be a vital and necessary part of medical practice—the very art of medicine.[39]

Soul and divinity:

The soul is our divine, *transpersonal* Self, the essence of who we are, covered by the persona of the ego. It is the *higher Self.* As it is transpersonal, it reaches *across and beyond the ego* to the eternal, infinite, divine nature of the spirit. When we discover this essence we come into the presence of the Source of all being—the Creator and Its Creation, inseparable. In the presence of our Source, we learn that we are not accidents governed by the so-called laws of chance, but vital parts of the living Universe. Furthermore, accidents seem to lie at the ends of long chains of circumstances—they are often the effect of a remarkably intricate set of causes. If you were to do some mathematical calculations of accidents where intersections of two moving objects are involved, the precision with which they meet has to be measured, at times, in thousandths of a second! I do not see how we can continue to believe in coincidences due to blind chance.

This statement can evoke many powerful reactions, especially from those people who have been involved in serious, harmful accidents. As I look back at my life, I see these intricacies in every accident or coincidence in my life, and as I look further into each of them, I find an important lesson for me in every one of them. I have exercised the divinely assured freedom of choice to see the opportunity to learn a lesson in every one of my accidents or mistakes. I am free of guilt and fully responsible for all of my thoughts and their associated actions. H.O.P.E. Group participants often express the same sensibilities once they have learned to look at their lives without guilt and to take responsibility for them. H.O.P.E. Group participants focus on finding meaning and value in their lives and come to make sense of such life-changing events[40].

SoulCircling workshops (Chapter 7) are condensed H.O.P.E. Group experiences that begin by asking participants to make a chronological list of events that have shaped their lives. We ask SoulCirclers to tell their stories to their SoulCircle, which is a "small group" that is essential to the SoulCircling process. Sad, painful happenings stand out in every list, and it is not uncommon for a participant to recognize that such an event is critical to where s-he is in her or his life. A frequently heard complaint in such circumstances is, "I wonder how I could possibly have done that?"

The group is encouraged to respond with, "Have you asked your soul lately?"

The eternal soul, preceding and succeeding each individual life, comes to find truth and love. We have certainly made many mistakes in our lives, both individually and collectively, and the soul's work is to make lessons out of the ego's mistakes. The soul's ways of going from mistakes to lessons—from problems to possibilities—are far more powerful than the ego's ability to control things. With eternity on its side, a soul can direct more than one lifetime to learning the lesson. It seems today that our souls have devoted many lifetimes to this learning, and now we move, under our soul's direction, toward one of the great transformations of our species and our world.

Indeed, the historically rich concepts of soul are currently rushing back into our consciousness. Book sellers enlarge their sections on spirituality to make room for books about soul written by physicists, theologians, and psychologists, to name but a few of the professions (re-)discovering soul. The word alone occurs in about 2000 book titles, and it is the topic of some 200 books. The popularity of many of these works provides a strong commentary on today's growing emphasis on the importance of finding our soul. If you have not read any yet, I suggest you pay a visit to the spirituality section of your local bookseller and see if a book jumps off the shelf at you. This is not an accident, but a spiritual grace note. The soul always works in such grace notes and the soul of its author wants to be close to your soul. It would appear that Soul found its way out of the brain and, once again, encompasses our entire being.

Soul and the feminine aspects of life

As I previously pointed out (p. 53), the soul's inherent qualities of passion, feeling, relating, sharing, and tenderness are feminine[41]. These qualities are complex patterns of images that reside in the right, feminine brain. They do not lend themselves well to the linear functions of reason and analysis that reside in the left, masculine brain. They are difficult to analyze, and the dominant male paradigm of social thought in which we have lived for thousands of years fears them because it cannot understand them. Little wonder that the male minds of the Enlightenment, working in the dominator model, rejected this powerful feminine aspect of human spirituality.

The Enlightenment intellectuals made passion and feeling insignificant by placing them under the control of the masculine mind. Most of the major religions of the world had long before debased the feminine body, making room for science, the youngest religion[42], and product of the masculine mind, to focus on the body as an object. Indeed, medicine, the youngest science,[43] taught me that the body is a molecular machine! As a tragic result of this kind of thinking, billions of us have grown up in high-tech, low-touch, ego-rich, soul-poor societies whose heart-less minds have no conscious awareness of their own soul. We are feeling a pain today that comes from this masculine-mind, ego-directed life, the pain of meaninglessness that we express in all of our abusive behaviors from our inwardly directed addictions to our outwardly directed violence. As we continue this way, so we threaten our very survival. When we choose to follow the pain rather than to try to numb it or give it away, we shall bring together mind and heart, ego and soul, and discover the joy of being alive.

The mystic, Antoine de St. Exupéry, said, "It is only with the heart that one can see rightly. What is essential is invisible to the eye."[44] When we blind the eye of the heart, our soul, we allow our minds to corrupt thought, and we misapply our knowledge.[45] Without heart, the mind is capable of dehumanizing people. All "ethnic cleansing" arises from dehumanized thought and its actions. We need our souls to guide us back to love, the way of the heart. We must remember that soul never left us; we left it. It is time we return to it, remembering that soul's home is the heart; its attitude is love; and its function is compassion and forgiveness.

Finding the soul's purpose:

Reflect now on the idea that your soul carries with it the reason for your existence here on earth… the reason that gives your life meaning[46]. It came here to occupy a specific physical form—yours—with its inherited qualities of talent and temperament, and to experience the way that you deal with the circumstances in which you find yourself. It did not come to live in isolation inside your brain. It came to gather specific knowledge and create a unique experience from it—your work. Your work is your soul's calling. It came here to write a once-told tale in the annals of the Universe. It came here to encompass your entire life with its love—to experience how you love, were loved, and showed others the way to love.

It came here knowing why it came, but the circumstances of your early life made you forget why you came; you were simply too busy trying to find your place in this world to remember who you really are. Your soul, in its eternal wisdom, chose to move into the background and become invisible to your ego. You forgot your work, and your ego's perceived needs directed you to find a job— the reflection of its need to control. A cloud of ego's perception came across the shining of your soul's vision and dimmed your sight. God made this necessary in order for us to learn the horribly destructive capabilities of the isolated and isolating, separated and separating, controlled and controlling ego. We are to learn to commit the ego's strength to the service of the power-full soul that in turn serves the all-powerful Creation.

The supreme challenge of a lifetime is first to convince the ego of the existence and presence of the soul and second to encourage it to move into a dynamic relationship with the soul. This relationship will make it possible for you to bring your job and your work close together. It will not matter that you work as a floor sweeper in a knitting mill or function as its CEO. The floor sweeper may be an angel who touches other lives with love and the CEO may develop a loving home care program for the workers' families. In such lovely, creative moments, the cloud disappears from the face of The Shining One, and Its light of truth illuminates the landscape of our lives and shows us the way Home.

Soul: a holographic fragment of Creation:

We have life because God is Life. The Life is in us, and we are in It. It is us but we are not It. We are but fragments of It… holographic fragments, and every soul is a holographic fragment of the soul of the Universe.

Lasers have given us the remarkable images called holograms[47], three-dimensional pictures that seem to be suspended in space, and visible as such from virtually every angle. If we cut up the film that contains the hologram and shine the laser through any one of the fragments, the image of the hologram remains intact. The smaller the fragment is, though, the fuzzier is the image.

"Holographic fragment" is a useful metaphor for the nature of a soul... it is a fully dimensioned image of God's experience. As a fragment, it can only be a fuzzy representation of God, yet The Beloved fully manifests Itself in the fragment. This spiritual metaphor for life shows us the way to an empowering psychology that brings meaning, value, and purpose to any life. Indeed, when people hold steadfast to this awareness in face of great challenges, they frequently appear in special segments of the evening news.

Sacred time, sacred art:

The soul lives only in the sacred time of the present moment. Secular time comprises the historical past and the mysterious future—the time of memory and projection—time that does not exist except in the thinking of the linear, masculine ego[48]. When we choose to live in the present moment, we choose to live in God's time. In the time of the Beloved, we make our lives a collaboration of our personal ego and individual soul. In this way, our lives become lives of service of the universal spirit—consecrated lives. We become one-of-a-kind treasures of sacred art.

A soul's journey begins in the glorious, passionate birth of the stars. It continues through their forming and reforming in what we call "death and rebirth." It is a sacred journey of Spirit alive in Body. When the cosmic soul came from the pure, clean fire of the first star, it split into a multitude of fragments that forever remembered their divine source as they formed more stars and their planets. That soul swam the primordial seas with the first single-celled organisms. It aggregated into the first multicellular organism when single-celled organisms clung together for a reason that soul knew but they did not. The new forms became more complex, creating organs with specific, vital functions. Thus, the cosmic soul gave birth to the incredible range of complex beings with organs of propulsion, digestion, sensation, circulation, excretion, reproduction, memory, communication, etc. The memory of our time in the spawning stars remains with us since the beginning and calls us back to that glorious moment of Being whose sound is not a "big bang," but the passionate symphony of uproarious, joyful, divine laughter.

Each one of us writes a unique life story, a single volume in an encyclopedia of the experience of one soul. Each volume of every encyclopedia is an essential part of the Creation Story, itself. The Story contains no errors. Were there but one infinitesimally small flaw, The Story would be imperfect, and, lacking in integrity, it would have winked out of existence, unable to sustain itself. The Creation Story can only be perfect. Its component parts can only be perfect, also. However, with our current belief in our imperfect nature, we convince ourselves that we are not a part if It. Certainly, a huge part of the great challenge before us is to appreciate what God means by "perfect".

(Re)discovering the passion of being has helped many of my patients heal. Exploring it with them brought us into a healthy, intimate relationship in which we discovered each other—as human beings. We had met each other first as persons and then as spiritual beings. Indeed, as I have said before and will repeat often, we are spiritual beings who are living a human experience, not human beings simply trying to find a spiritual experience. The name of our spiritual being is "soul." The discovery and realization of the soul's intent in coming here heals us, even though our so-called illness may not be cured.

Body, mind, soul, and spirit:

In many ways, mind resembles spirit. In many ways, body resembles soul. As we reach out to our spiritual nature, the mind evolves into the spirit and the body evolves into the soul. In short, we transcend our old, limited nature and discover the wonder of a creative life without limits.

The discovery of neuropeptides has revealed the connections between the mind and the body. Candace Pert, Ph.D., calls the neuropeptides molecules of emotion[49]. These remarkable chemicals render feelings tangible and measurable—they are part of the tangible soul. They reflect the state of the emotional, feeling part of our brain called the limbic system, whose clusters of specialized nerve cells provide an emotional evaluation of every thought that flows from the cortices of our brains to the muscles and organs of our body. They also provide a similar evaluation of every sensory experience of our bodies that flows into our cerebral cortices. Every emotion has a chemical component; complex emotions evoke constellations of these chemicals. Every cell in our bodies has receptors for these chemicals. Moreover, our bodies elaborate many if not all of them in organs other than the brain, releasing them from the organ into the bloodstream that carries them to the brain! In this way, every single cell becomes aware of every feeling, informed by either the nervous system or the circulatory system. Feelings inform our selves of how our minds and organs are doing… they inform our *being.*

Of the many neuropeptides and their emotions, only two are necessary for raw, immediate survival: fear and its stepchild, anger.[50] Because of their importance, the ego uses these emotions to protect us from harm and *thinks* it is essential to life. Love, on the other hand, *is* essential to life and is capable of taking the projection out of fear and anger and turning them into awareness and presence.[51] It is difficult to convince the ego of this because of its orientation to fear. Love is the attitude of spiritual life common to all great religions. This single attitude contains a remarkable constellation of emotions that evaluate our life-giving experiences: happiness, joy, bliss, serenity, and inner peace—the emotions of the soul. Today, ever more people are becoming aware of the wonder of experiencing these emotions. This awareness leads us out of the way of ego and into the way of soul.

Science has reduced the Universe to a huge collection of atoms circulating according to fixed, impersonal laws. Its analytical, objective approach to reality went so far as to make mind the product of physico-chemical reactions, removing it from the rule of love that flows from the heart. Thinking only with the mind has horribly addicting properties. Addictions are harmful substitutes for love that bypass the heart and lead us into all misapplications of knowledge—the same unfettered masculine, mental approach that made possible the impersonal and inhuman murder of Jews, Gypsies, political prisoners, and homosexuals by Hitler and his Nazi thugs, the modern equivalent of the rapacious, murdering hordes of Genghis Khan.

The marriage of body and mind, ego and soul:

The great Sufi mystic, Jalaluddin Rumi (1207-1273 CE), experienced the shift from intellectualism and reason to intuition and ecstasy and wrote about it. He found the way of the heart to have its own addicting potential in the tremendous power of the ecstatic high. This addiction was not likely to cause others harm; it merely took a human away from his ground to a state in which the human would lose all effectiveness. He stressed, as did those Sufi mystics who came for 600 years before and after him, that the way of the heart was not to negate the way of the mind, but that the two were to work together in balanced relationship. The resulting balance would be, as he put it, the Perfect Man.

Whereas the ego believes that might makes right and that judging is a power that reflects might, the soul knows what is right without needing to judge anything. Consider that the soul uses that word, "right," as Buddhists use it in their eight-fold path[52]. That which is "right" brings the fundamental law by which the universe functions (dharma) to human awareness and application. When we choose to follow this path, it takes us beyond the causes of all of our suffering to a "Self" that is more a witness than a director. That Self is our soul, which sees all things in the truth of their relationships to each other. Our soul is on familiar terms with the dharma, for it is our conscience—that which chooses right over wrong. As Thomas Merton said, "Conscience is the face of soul."[53] The simple and yet profound truth in these words sing deeply inside of me, touching *my* soul.

Soul

When people ask me about the soul, I like to tell them that soul lies at the heart of everything, encompassing the entire body-mind, including the ego. Coming here with "earth orders" it is the captain of the ship of life who more observes the passage of that ship than directs it, for the manifest is already written in the stars. What matters is the experience of the journey, but in our world of intellectualism, the ego does not know that. It believes it is in complete control of the ship—the captain-navigator. It does not know that the soul is a piece of the ever-present divine Spirit that comes here to be an individual who creates a unique volume of life's experiences. The soul is, then, the essence of any one life, whereas the spirit is the source of all life; and, as the soul encompasses an individual body-mind, so the spirit encompasses that body-mind-soul.

Soul and personality:

Each soul comes into a genetic environment that contains all of the elements of personality [54] (p. 29). The physical being that will be its home will be born into a family which will respond to its gifts of personality with their own personalities. In this way, the environment of the older persons will begin to exercise an influence on the form, thought, and behavior of the new human, creating a new individual[55]. If that environment is ego-centered, it will try to control the newcomer. If it is soul-centered, it will empower the newcomer.

Soul and creativity:

Our soul comes through to our consciousness in many ways. The soul of a playwright comes through to us in his plays. The soul of a mother comes through to us in her nurturance. The soul of a composer comes through to us in his compositions. The soul of an artist comes through to us in her landscapes. The soul of a mason comes through to us in the fine lines and balance of his arches and walls. The soul of a teacher comes through to us in how she helps us inform our lives. The soul of a physician comes through to us in his healing ministry. The soul of a worker comes through to us in the quality of the product of her work. The soul of a portraitist comes through to us in his brilliant ability to portray the soul of his subject in the painting.

When a skilled musician plays a composition written by someone long dead, the soul of that musician joins with the soul of the composer, and the resulting product is a distinctive, wondrous performance. When you listen to Herbert von Karajan conduct the Berlin Symphonic Orchestra in a performance of one of Johann Sebastian Bach's Brandenburg Concertos, you hear something that has different qualities than when Rudolf Baumgartner conducts the Festival Strings Lucerne performing the same concerto. They are both stunning performances, and, in both cases, the soul of the eighteenth century composer comes through to the listener. More-over, it comes through with the coloring of the soul of the twenti-eth century conductor and his orchestra. Their souls are in what we hear and not in the plastic compact disk or the CD player that pro-duces the sound by "reading" the disk. The interaction of disk and player faithfully reproduce the performance and thus bring us the passionate expression of *all* of the souls involved.

The soul of the performance lies in the spacing and power of the notes. Bach's soul shaped the vertical intervals between the notes that make up chords and the horizontal intervals between the chords. Herbert von Karajan's soul adds an interpretation to Bach's composition that changes the power of Bach's chords and their horizontal intervals ever so slightly—yet ever so signifi-cantly. Rudolf Baumgartner's soul adds yet another dimension to Bach's composition—and my appreciation of Bach's soul grows when I hear this new performance.

The great men and women of music pour their souls out to us in their work. We are likely to say of them that they were in-spired, which means they let the spirit in (and remember, please, that inspire means to breathe in)! Wolfgang Amadeus Mozart would have a complete symphony come to him in an instant—as an image—and then he would struggle to write it all down in a spe-cialized symbolic language of wiggles and squiggles, lines and

dots called musical notation. When architects, designers, mathema-
ticians, and physicists work at their peak, they all receive a single
image in an instant that they proceed to describe in terms of their
own specialized symbolic languages. They, too, were inspired.
Where do these images come from: ego-driven men or soul-
directed human beings responding to spirit's presence? Let "inspired" speak for itself.

It is neither necessary nor desirable to limit the phenomenon of "inspired" to a few chosen people. Consider taking that
word back to its source. Was God not wonderfully inspired to create the Universe? Then everything in It is the result of that inspiration, including you and me. That makes each of us both composer
and conductor of a symphony of Universal value and meaning. The
notes and intervals of our music come to us from the whole Universe—from the pen of the greatest Composer of all—just as they
did for Mozart. The work that you and I are here to do flows from
soul of the Universe as an unencumbered gift to our own soul's
creativity. God has given us both of this divine Gift to interpret
based on our experience of It. Each of us composes and conducts a
unique, one-of-a-kind performance of a symphony dedicated to the
very existence of the Universe!

Soul and eternity:

"(Soul) often is considered to survive the death of the
body" (Encyclopedia Britannica, op. cit.). This fifth quality of Soul
speaks to its ability to endure beyond the limits of time, as we
know it. If that property of soul is, indeed, real, then logic and reason have to step aside in favor of intuition—the way of the heart.
You are familiar with my arguments for this shift (p. 64)

Enamored as we are of technology, we must keep in mind
that, no matter how advanced it may be, it remains an extension of
our sensible minds. Intuition, on the other hand, is not related to
our senses. Rather, it "is the perception or comprehension, as of
truths or facts, without the use of the rational process (American
Heritage Dictionary op. cit.)." It is often referred to as "direct

knowledge." Albert Einstein is supposed to have said, "None of my discoveries were the product of my rational mind." His non-rational mind was his way of understanding the non-rational universe. If I say, "The universe is a point of light within the mind of God[56]," we can only appreciate the meaning of that statement with our non-rational minds. We must use this mind in order to understand and appreciate this fifth quality of soul.

Whereas reason tells us that there is no evidence of a "soul" that occupies a series of human bodies, intuition appreciates the anecdotal story of the little girl who asked her baby brother to tell her about God because she was "beginning to forget (p. 8)." That same intuition can lead us to appreciate the work of scientifically trained professionals like Raymond A. Moody, Ph.D., M.D., Kenneth Ring, Ph.D., and Brian Weiss, M.D., all of whom have written eloquently about their experiences with people who have either experienced life before their life or after it. Each of them heard stories from their clients/patients that challenged their scientific, rational minds to the core. These experiences led them to an awareness of that non-rational, mystical nature of life that is the life of a soul.

People in H.O.P.E. Groups have similar stories. About the time that I started this work, I heard the mystical statement: "we choose our parents." My rational, scientific mind rejected this out of hand. The remarkable stories I subsequently heard left me shaking my head in confusion until it all began to make intuitive sense. When it did, I understood the Zen koan, "What was the nature of your face before your parents were born?"

Soul and the heart:

As I mentioned above, our senses are limited. Our eyes are sensitive to an extremely narrow range of electromagnetic radiation. We cannot see in the ultraviolet or infrared ranges as can quite a number of other living things. Even if we could, the remaining and invisible part of the spectrum would still be huge. Our hearing is also limited. We cannot hear the hyposonic communication of elephants or the hypersonic sonar of bats. With our limited perceptions of the physical universe, we cannot sense it rightly. To see something rightly, Antoine de St. Exupéry counsels us to see it with our hearts (p. 59). Why the heart? The answer lies in the origins of the Latin and Greek root words for heart… *cor* and *kardia*, respectively. The former evolves into the French word *coeur* and the latter evolves into the English-Germanic word *heart*. The heart is at the core of human experience and we can consciously hold all of our core experience in our hearts. The choice to use our hearts is ours as a divine gift, and it may be the most important choice that we have to make in our lives.

In spite of our limited senses, defining things has long been one of the great seductions and addictions of rational minds. Defining literally and figuratively demands that we impose limits on the object that we define—that we "take its measure." Limiting some things with definitions helps us understand them, but certain things, like The Divine, defy limits. It is impossible to define or put limits on God.[57] It is impossible to define The Mystery or any of its expressions such as love, grace, truth, life, and soul. However, although we may not be able to define them, we can write down our thoughts about and experiences of them—describe them.

With all that I have said before from my non-rational mind, I offer you this *description* of soul:

> In the beginning, Spirit utters Its One Commandment, "Be!" and Soul cries out, "I am!" proclaiming itself a unique reflection of that magnificent utterance—a bridge between the finite, temporal universe and the infinite, eternal universe. Soul has qualities long-eliciting considerable interest from religion and philosophy: It is loving and kind; passionate and compassionate; patient and shy; courageous and persistent. It is an instrument of creativity and transformation, a non-judgmental energy moving effortlessly through space and time gathering experience of unfathomable, universal value. It is the essence of life.

Chapter 4: "Out of Body"

Principles:

- Trauma fragments the soul.
- The soul dissociates under a host of circumstances.
- Reincarnation makes healing possible.
- Soul-workers (shamans) have been around for millennia.

Eternal soul in temporal body:

Five important soul phenomena have appeared in our Western experience in the last quarter of the 20th century: fragmentation of the soul; out-of-body experiences, with or without a near-death experience (NDE); reincarnation, especially in respect to past life regression therapy; shamanic practices; and visits from beyond. A grasp of these concepts will help us to understand more about the soul.

Life is far more than ashes-to-ashes, dust-to-dust existence. Mother Earth gives us the ashes and dust of our physical bodies. They flow through us like water, renewing the atomic body about every fourteen months. The body's inherent wisdom directs this flow of matter, sustaining its patterns for years, maintaining the home of the soul through the process we call aging.[58] Only the incarnate soul that lives the sacred life can fully appreciate the value of the entire process; the ego, living the secular, finite life, cannot.

However, the butterfly-like fragility of the soul makes it shy and retiring. This fragility is its strength: a true tenderness, rich in compassion, and an exquisite sensitivity to its circumstances. Being eternal, it has the power to outwait the suffering of its temporal home, the body. Indeed, the suffering may be so great that the soul knows that healing will take more than one lifetime to complete. So be it, the time is not important; the experience of healing is.

Fragmenting the soul, having a piece of your soul leave home:

The soul's fragility makes it subject to wounding. Because we are at best only faintly conscious of the soul's presence, we are hardly aware that a soul can be wounded, let alone how it would respond to the wounding. A soul can suffer a wound from any kind of trauma, even a sprained ankle, but none is more egregious than when a naked, soul-less ego—a Hitler—traumatizes and fragments another person's soul out of a craving to restore its own lost soul. Such soul-less human deeds make ugly front-page news items.

Soul-aware societies[59], the world over, share an awareness of soul's tenderness and sensitivity to trauma. Trauma causes breaks or gaps in the integrity of the soul, and the soul *fragments.* It breaks off the injured piece in order for it to find safety from the trauma. As "civilized" societies today navigate almost exclusively under the direction of their secular, separated egos, they see these soul gaps as weaknesses and develop defenses that hide them in a dark part of our minds called the *shadow*. Losing those parts of our soul damages the integrity of the soul, and we lose our natural sense of wholeness. Not being whole, we cannot be healthy, for health and wholeness mean essentially the same thing, coming as they both do from the old Germanic word root, *hael*.

When my aunt "rescued" me from my "stupid" clam-digging adventure (p. 35), the terror I felt caused a part of me to disassociate from the rest of me and stay under the water, where it was safe from her terrified and terrifying anger. That tender part of my soul had lived the "stupid" metaphors in other lifetimes and was asking for this life to heal that wound. It knew it would have to wait fifty years for the opportunity, but that was insignificant in contrast to the years it had already spent on the project.

I paid a tremendous price for this loss and my ego did its best to compensate for it. It wrote that set of life rules that it believed would protect me from such insults. However, they were not adequate for all of the demands that life would impose, nor were they adequate to resist the pressure of my soul to recover its lost

71

part. The soul part of my self patiently, subtly, ingeniously, and inexorably set up situations in which it hoped to be able to recover that piece and be whole—to heal. As I mentioned above (p. 39), I would suddenly find myself doing something unbelievably stupid for which I would be discovered and accused of my worst fear—stupidity. In the face of my accuser, I would become speechless and helpless, no matter how well I might have rehearsed my responses. My accuser would get the strangest look of confusion on his or her face, shrug, and turn away, muttering. I would slowly come back from this strange, confused state and damn myself for being stupid.

These strange behaviors are the essentials of the posttraumatic stress disorder (PTSD). My "stupid" actions were a dysfunctional behavior in that they caused harm to self or others. Fortunately, I never seriously harmed anyone. Having disassociated in my helpless, speechless state, I was not home; I had become that terrified child who left a part of himself under the waters of Great Peconic Bay looking peacefully up at the lovely ripples. I had repressed all memory of the rescue in order to protect myself from the abject terror I had felt when grabbed from behind. Try as I might, especially when my mother reminded me of the incident, I had never been able to remember anything beyond looking up from my raking and seeing silvery ripples in the water overhead.

I am deeply grateful for the fact that my mother told me many times how her sister had run into the water in her best summer dress to rescue me from drowning. I knew of the incident only vicariously until I relived it as an adult. My experience removes any doubt from my mind that repressed memories do exist. However, not all are as fortunate as I am to have had a witness to the trauma.

Three things are certain for me in my experience: one, I experienced complete release from the terror when I recovered the memory. Two, I bore no ill will toward my aunt. Three, the dysfunctional behavior and its related dissociation never returned.

There has been a lot of discussion about the validity of recovering repressed memories… innocent people have been hurt.

When I do any form of regressive work with people, and I tell them that unless the memory recovery results in compassionate forgiveness of the entire situation and relief from dysfunctional behavior, *that* memory is not reliable. I advise people to trust only those memories that bring relief of symptoms and provide the ability to let the remembered perpetrator go—in peace.

People who have experienced terrifying, traumatic circumstances commonly display these disordered, dissociative behaviors. They have lost a part of their soul to the trauma and have repressed the memories. In 1987, when I recovered the memory of the clam-digging episode, I felt my aunt's hands around my chest. I heard and felt the water cascade off me as I came up out of the water. I felt myself spun around and shaken like a rat in a terrier's mouth. I saw into her eyes and mouth as she screamed, "You stupid little boy!" I knew I was remembering being terrified beyond my ability to imagine terror. As trying as that memory was in 1987, it was nowhere near as horrible as it had been to the little boy in 1937. I had gone though the trauma without being re-traumatized. Such is not always the case, though, and there are ways of recovering lost soul fragments without revisiting the suffering that caused the loss, as we shall see later.

The third aspect of the experience was a wonder of wonders! Never again would I set up a situation in which the old dysfunctional behavior recurred! Never again would I dissociate in the face of another person's anger! The relief has been profound, and I am at peace with my memories of my aunt, whereas a constant undertone of tension always colored our relationship while she was alive.

This peacefulness and forgiveness are not ready functions of the ego. Rather, they are functions of the soul, which is, after all, "that part of an individual which partakes of divinity." The ego's tools for survival are fear and anger, avoidance and attack. To seek retribution—to punish—is an ego-function that only perpetuates the trauma. To look at the perpetrator through the soft eyes of compassion makes forgiveness possible and leads to peace.

Such peace used to be "the peace of God" that passes "beyond all human understanding". Not any more… we are getting it!

Out-of-Body Experiences, when the unfragmented soul leaves home:

Out-of-body experiences take place in altered states of consciousness and when the body experiences extreme physical or emotional trauma. We all experience the former in our dreams, those rich, visual, auditory, tactile, and kinesthetic images that we all experience three or four times nightly, whether we remember them or not. We can come away from dreamtime believing the experience was real. People who have passed on come to us in dreams. We receive important instructions in dreams. Problems solve themselves in dreams. We encounter meaningful legendary figures and experiences in dreams. We visit The Mystery in dreams, as psychologists and psychiatrists are well aware. For many indigenous cultures, dreamtime is a time for the soul to wander, and they wake a person from sleep very carefully lest the soul not have fully returned to the body by the time of full awakening. Dreams are soul-journeys.

An out-of-body experience in the awakened state can put a person in contact with people and situations from other times even when death has separated them. Toward the end of the last century, out-of-body experiences became the subject of many books and popular media experiences. The ones with the greatest popular appeal took place in situations where the person came close to dying. Raymond A. Moody[60] described the experiences of many of his counseling clients who had such experiences when their lives where threatened. They all moved through a long dark tunnel towards a point of brilliant light only to meet a presence at or near the end of the tunnel who told them that their time had not come and that they were to return to the body. Kenneth Ring[61] described the experiences of people who went all the way into the light at the end of this tunnel. There they were in the presence of beings whom they could sometimes see and sometimes not. Most of them received instructions as to what they were to do with their lives.

Dannion Brinkley[62] and Elizabeth J. Eadie[63] have both written about their remarkable experiences of being clinically dead for considerable periods of time, during which they were in the presence of "beings" that instructed them as to the nature of the work of their soul. Both have been following these instructions ever since.

All of these anecdotes seem to support the view that the existence of the soul extends beyond the body in both time and space. These stories are so convincing, and so many writers of excellent reputation have described them that it is virtually impossible to simply pass off the experience as an hallucination or a condition of the brain caused by a lack of oxygen or a surge of happiness-producing brain chemicals.

I would like to share with you some stories that came to me directly from the person involved:

An out-of-body experience without an NDE:

A woman in her thirties had experienced two recurrences of a difficult cancer. Her doctors had told her there was still cancer in her body, and they were proposing more therapies. She had been through considerable physical trials with the others, and, as trying as they had been, she wanted to access and develop as much of her own resources as possible before taking part in further medical therapy. She wanted to make it work.

She was attracted to a weekend retreat with a healer who worked with music. There, she found she could enter deep meditative states while listening to his music. In one of these states, she found herself out of her body, going down a long dark tunnel toward a beautiful, brilliant, yet comfortable light. She went into the light and knew that she was in the presence of beings that she could not see. They spoke to her without voices, yet she understood them clearly. They gave her instructions about what she was to do with her life. She began to follow them to the letter, and was still in good health, many years later.

Another woman with severe musculo-skeletal pain from several accidents was studying brainwave biofeedback with a psychologist. She found relief in this work, and started to find herself in strange, yet pleasant and reassuring places when she attained certain levels of relaxation. One session was moving along pleasantly when she suddenly found herself out of her body, traveling down a long, dark tunnel toward a lovely, brilliant light that did not hurt her eyes. She burst out into that light and found herself in the presence of the four adults in her family who had subjected her to much physical and emotional abuse as she was growing up. They had all died years before, and now they welcomed her with a peace and love that stunned her, transforming huge amounts of the anger with which she had lived most of her life. On returning to ordinary reality, she realized she still had the pain, but its griping edge had blunted and softened. Her attitude had also changed from that sharp edge of anger to a softness of inner peace.

An out-of-body experience in an NDE:

A remarkable woman brought her near-death experience (NDE) to an early H.O.P.E. Group meeting of sixteen people, all of whom had cancer. This woman came in a few minutes after the meeting had begun. The group members were already checking in with their experiences of the preceding week. We grew quiet while she sat down and then made her welcome by introducing ourselves. We asked her if she would like to introduce herself. She responded by saying that she was not sure why she had come to this group because she did not have cancer. She only had terrible pain in her body from multiple fractures that she sustained in an automobile accident that happened when her husband inadvertently pulled away from a stop sign into the path of a truck.

The first thing she became aware of after the accident was that she was in a hospital emergency room… but she was not in her body. She was "floating" just below the ceiling looking down at doctors and nurses working on her body lying on a stretcher. Her husband's body was on another stretcher with a crowd of doctors and nurses around it and he was "floating" up under the ceiling with her. What was even more remarkable about this was that they were with her father who had been dead for ten years and her husband's mother who had been dead for eight years! All four were wordlessly communicating with each other about what was going on. She told us that, after a while, her husband said, "I've done all the work I came here to do. I'm not going back," to which her response was, "I've not done all my work, so I am going back."

She then said that in the next instant, she was back in her body with excruciating pain in all of her broken bones. She knew her husband was gone and about ten minutes later the doctors pulled a sheet over her his face. She ended this remarkable story by saying, "I wonder why I came back. The pain has been terrible and I miss him so badly." Sixteen people with cancer knew why she had come back, and they responded with deep gratitude for her story and her presence.

Had you been there, her strength and peacefulness would have impressed you; as they did the others. The people to whom she told this story were intelligent and clear-minded. They were intent on learning as much as they could about what they could do with their lives in face of their serious, potentially life-threatening diseases. She was absent from the next week's meeting, and we spent the first few minutes talking about her, her story, and its value for us. No one doubted its truth. It had affected everyone deeply and positively. One person said he thought he now knew the meaning of synchronicity because her visit came at just the right time in his life. Another said she felt she had received a direct experience of grace.

This woman—this angel—never came back and we realized that she had never given us her name! However, her story lingers on. I have repeated it hundreds of times to people concerned about their own death and dying. Wherever she may be, I hope she knows how many people feel deeply grateful for the gift of her knowledge and experience of the continuity of life.

Reincarnation

Up until the beginning of the 18th century, reincarnation had been a part of Judaic, Christian, and Islamic belief. In addition, European societies up to that time had recognized soul, the active principle in reincarnation, as an essential component of human life along with the body, mind, and spirit. However, as I pointed out above (p. 53), scientific reason at that time discarded the soul; it seems that it never left us.

Brian Weiss, MD, is a psychiatrist who met the idea of the reincarnation of the soul in a series of remarkable encounters with a patient who was suffering from eleven different phobias, each with its own panic attacks.[64] As they worked together under hypnosis, she experienced the traumatic death of each of eleven different people living in eleven different times. Each experience of dying bore a relationship to one of her phobias and its associated panic attacks. In each instance, she experienced the profound peace common to all who go out of body, and both the phobia and its panic attack completely disappeared on coming out of trance. His experience supports the shamanic (q.v.) perception that a traumatic death may hold the soul in non-ordinary reality instead of releasing it to incarnate into another human still in its mother's womb. The consequences of such soul entrapment reach out over time causing illnesses that relate to the mechanism of death. The trapped soul seeks ways to attract the attention of healers who will set it free to resume its incarnations and experiences of life.

Weiss' experiences and those of his patient help us examine the validity of believing in the eternal nature of the soul. The person living in "ordinary" Western thinking is commonly discouraged from birth to have any curiosity about mysterious things. The mysterious, mystical experience has for the last two or three hundred years largely been the sole property of prophets, psychics and seers. The Universe presents us now with circumstances and situations that ask us to take a new look at our perception of life. Through these powerful stories, The Great Mystery presents us with evidence of Its existence. It is asking us to look inward to the phenomenon of the soul and its mysteries. My personal and vicarious experiences strongly suggest that our illnesses and dysfunctions are associated with wounds of the soul that go back in time into the collective of human experience.

What might it be, other than the soul, that goes out of body down a long tunnel and into a brilliant light to either return or leave? As I examine our descriptions of the soul, the higher Self, I find they clarify this aspect of the Mystery. If you still question the remarkable properties of the soul, read the following story told by a woman in another H.O.P.E. Group who worked as a hospice volunteer in regional nursing homes. She told us about being present to the dying of a tiny little old woman who had a wonderfully clear mind and a terribly weak heart.

One day, while she was paying a hospice visit to the old woman, the older one suddenly said, "Get in bed with me and hold me, I'm going!" No sooner had she done as asked, than the tired old heart stopped beating. The H.O.P.E.'r held her center, remaining peaceful. Suddenly, she found herself walking across a prairie towards a river, carrying her little friend who, to her surprise, was alive and alert! The H.O.P.E.'r has never seen the prairie, let alone walked in it, and yet she knew exactly where she was! She could feel the prairie grasses brushing against her calves and the gentle breeze in her face carrying its beautiful bouquet of prairie grasses and flowers. As they approached the river, the H.O.P.E.'r could see that there was a small crowd of people approaching from the other side.

Her tiny burden suddenly cried out, "Jennifer! Is that you?" whereupon one of the group stepped forward and called, "Yes, Gram, it's me. How are you?" The old one replied, "I'm fine, but how are you? You died ten years ago, didn't you?" to which the answer came, "Yes, and I'm fine. It's wonderful to see you, Gram!"

One by one, the others in the group came forward and greeted the little woman in my friend's arms as they continued to approach the river. They were all family members or close friends who had died earlier. When the two reached the river, there was no visible way across, so the little one called out, "How do we get across?" "Keep walking!" was the reply. They turned and walked along the river while the conversations continued. Twice more they asked how to get across. The first time they were told to keep walking, but the second time they were told to look ahead of them... there was a bridge! The little one looked years younger as she said, "Take me halfway across and put me down." The H.O.P.E.'r did as she was asked. They said "goodbye" in the middle of that bridge and The H.O.P.E.'r turned back. Immediately, the prairie disappeared and she found herself in the bed in the nursing home, holding the lifeless body of her little friend!

This particular H.O.P.E.'r is a practical, down-to-earth woman who quietly tells this lovely story with a soft Maine accent. She kept it to herself for some time after the incident, concerned about what others might think. When she told it to her group, her eyes widened and glistened—and so did ours. Her voice filled with emotion as she told the tale, and she ended by saying that the experience had changed her views of life and death, giving her own life a new and powerful sense of meaning.

Shamans and Shamanism: Soul Retrievers:

Virtually every society around the world has or had soulworkers called shamans. The word comes from the Tungus people of Siberia. The word also has distinct ties to Sanskrit and Prakrit word sources, and the archeological evidence for their work goes back at least 40,000 years! They specialize in going into what Michael Harner, Ph.D.[65] calls "non-ordinary reality"[66] where they speak to souls to get stories, and retrieve soul fragments that dissociated because of trauma—and we thought psychotherapy began with Freud!

"Out of Body"

Shamans have the power to travel between the material and spiritual worlds. Mental or physical wounds commonly identify them, and in their village or tribe, these wounds are believed to give them their magical powers. They are perfect examples of *wounded healers*. It is not uncommon in these societies for a person with epilepsy or early-onset schizophrenia to be singled out for shamanic training.

Shamanic practices relate directly to experiences of the soul. The shaman learns to travel to non-ordinary realms of consciousness to visit the soul of the one for whom s-he journeys. In this way, s-he obtains valuable information for the object of her journey. In the case of a physical injury, the shaman may travel to find the injured part, and bring it "home" to the injured body.

Shamanic practices teach that fragmentation of the soul by physical, mental, or emotional trauma causes both physical and mental illness. PTSD, depression, and virtually all of the psychoses are examples of illnesses resulting from soul loss. The shaman recovers the separated fragments in non-ordinary reality and returns them to the soul of the person for whom s-he journeys. Ordinary reality, the pragmatic, nuts-and-bolts reality in which we move as we go about our daily lives, tends to exclude experiences of the mystery that surrounds our condition. We in the West have become so oriented to that material, measurable universe of ordinary reality that we find the non-material, immeasurable, mysterious universe confusing and even threatening. To protect ourselves, we tend to reject it from our perceptions. However, shamans routinely and safely visit this mysterious realm in their rituals.

A shaman performing soul retrieval enters into trance through a simple ritual usually accompanied by the beating of a drum or the rhythmical playing of an instrument such as a musical bow or a didgeridoo[67]. With the help of an animal spirit guide s-he travels to the time and place of the original wound where the lost soul fragment hides, and brings it back home. S-he ends her ritual by gently blowing the soul fragments into the heart and crown of the one for whom s-he has journeyed. S-he then welcomes the person home, and then s-he tells the person about her journey.

I learned soul retrieval from Sandra Ingerman[68]. Sandra introduced me to the use of the word, *essence,* to describe the soul; the same word several of my Buddhist acquaintances use for the soul. Sandra spent a significant amount of time with my training group making sure that we could come to appreciate that concept. Essence means, "being," the action of the commandment that we have seen before (p. 22). *Being* is an essential quality of living things[69], and, as we remember from earlier statements, the soul is the *immaterial being* (p. 50) of our lives. It is indeed our essence.

I often journey without knowing anything of a person's story… it makes for interesting surprises! Journeying one day for a man in his forties, I entered the moderate trance state I have come to identify with the shamanic journey, and found myself in a newborn nursery in a hospital, standing in front of an infant incubator. I saw myself opening it, lifting out its infant occupant, and saying to him, "I'm here to take you home," to which he replied, "It's about time you came. I'm ready!" (In non-ordinary reality newborn infants can speak). I returned to the ordinary reality of my office, and as I was going through the closing part of the ritual, the man suddenly began to weep. I waited, and when he was quiet, I asked him what had come up for him. He said he did not know, but it seemed that the most profound sense of relief had come over him. I told him then about my journey, and he wept again, deeply. He then told me that when he was born, his umbilical cord was wrapped twice around his neck, nearly strangling him. He had had to spend the first two weeks of his life in an incubator, away from his mother! He said that he had always had to work on deep, powerful feelings of abandonment. Subsequently, many harmful behaviors that had plagued him for most of his life just seemed to evaporate!

Our society preserves quite a number of rituals that make it possible for their practitioners to enter non-ordinary reality. Most of them are religious, taking place in the sanctuary of a church on a designated day of the week under the direction of a trained guide, usually ordained as a minister or priest. The rituals draw us into a trance state in which we visit non-ordinary reality. Once there, we get images that are just as real to us as the cars stopping and going at the traffic lights outside the church. Such religious rituals are directed at inducing states of consciousness that help access the Mystery, for which the members of a particular church or temple have a name. For an ecumenical shaman, that name might simply be "non-ordinary reality." For the churchgoer, that name might simply be "God." Whatever name we choose for the Mystery, it responds.

Visits from Beyond:

We can enrich our perceptions of the nature of the soul with the strange and wonderful stories of the visit of a dying person's soul to a beloved spouse or family member. Many people have had a direct or vicarious experience of this nature, and such accounts have been with us for hundreds of years. These visits are incredibly synchronous with the person's actual time of death and always deeply moving to the living who experience them.

A friend of mine lost her favorite brother to cancer while he was still in his thirties. As his illness progressed, it became necessary to admit him to a nursing home for long-term care. Acting out of her fondness for him, she made it a habit to visit him frequently after work. One evening, after one particularly loving and intimate visit, she drove home along a coastal road with which she was very familiar. As she approached a lighthouse that stood only 100 yards from the road, a pure white deer suddenly crossed the road right in front of her, forcing her almost to a stop. As it passed in front of her car, it turned its head, looked directly into her eyes, and then bounded off toward the lighthouse. Instantly, she knew that her brother had died, and even though everyone expected him to live for several more weeks! She went back to his nursing home and stunned the staff with her awareness of his death. When she told them of her encounter with the deer, the nurse who had been with him as he died turned pale and said, "His final words were, 'To the lighthouse!'"

When a soul liberates itself from the body that had been its home, what *are* its capabilities? How can it possibly manifest itself as an albino deer crossing a lonely country road in time to stop a beloved relative and send her back to the nursing home? Recall the story of the woman who was so badly injured in the auto accident in which her husband died (p. 77), and create a perception that time may not always be quite as it seems to be on a day-to-day basis. Where have the long-dead parents been while their children were living normal, human lives before that accident so suddenly interrupted them? Where were my parents all the time it took for me to get in touch with them on that misty morning in 1987? In addition, what about those beings, those souls, who were waiting, as it were, for the little, old woman The H.O.P.E.'r carried across the prairie to the river and the bridge to the other side?

The ancient Greeks had two concepts of time: *chronos* and *kairos*. Chronos is the linear time dimension of the physical universe that appeals to the ego. Kairos is the non-linear time dimension of the spiritual universe that appeals to the soul.

The ancient Celts had a deep appreciation of the spiritual universe that included a sense that there was a *veil* separating the physical and spiritual worlds. They sensed there were places where the veil thinned to give glimpses into the spiritual universe. Could it be that all these visits from beyond occur in places where the veil between the realm of the body and the realm of the spirit is so thin as to become transparent? Could it also be that the soul knows how to thin the veil? Could it also be that the discovery and experience of these remarkable phenomena leads us to the recovery of the soul of the human species?

Let us look at what this might mean for our hard-working egos.

Chapter 5: Homecoming

Life is not measured by the number of breaths we take,
but by the moments that take our breath away.... Your
ego can stop counting the breaths and join your soul in
the joy of such moments.

Author unknown

Principle:

- The team of the soul and the ego provides God with the experience of Its own life.

Where we have been and where we must go:

We have seen that life is the journey of a soul that comes here with the experience of other lifetimes to gather knowledge and create yet more experience of Universal value. In each lifetime, the soul collaborates with a different personality and its ego. Of necessity, the life of an ego is a life lived in varying degrees of separation and loneliness, pressured by time into a fear-limited box out of which every one of us continually strives to do better than others. What would it be like if the ego were to commit itself to work together with the soul?

Life repeatedly gives us the opportunity for this collaboration in our *crises*—our *dangerous opportunities* (p. 55). The ego looks for strengths that it can use to control or flee the danger and finds them in the "what"(s) of its life (p. 29). Without the soul's knowledge of the "who" of life that gives life meaning, the ego can only push its way through life, using its anger to get there.

However, the strength for all of this pushing usually peaks when a person is in her or his mid-twenties (along with her or his physical strength). It can only last for another ten or fifteen years. As the ego begins to fatigue, the soul, with eternity on its side, and love that puts everything in beneficial relationship, can now come forward to claim its birthright and guide the life through the crisis.

Success belongs to those who discover the way past a crisis. However, the quality of the success depends on that part of self which discovers the way. If the ego finds the way, it achieves *penultimate* success because it works in isolation and lacks the timeless, spiritual value of the experience. When the *soul* finds the way through the crisis, it achieves *ultimate* success, for it has chronicled the journey in the pages of eternity.

The soul path beyond the crisis goes through the valley of the shadow of death, where the ego fears to tread. The soul's experience of past lives demands that the path take it through the valley into *the dark night of the soul*. In these moments, the soul—ship's captain following its earth orders—asks the ego to lend its strengths to completing the task. If it has been fragmented, the soul will subtly direct the ego to seek the help of others to help it recover and integrate those fragments. They help the soul gather up its experience in collaboration with its navigator and write a story of universal value.

In 1975, I had a crisis of anger at just such an impasse… incredibly specific interactions at a stop sign on my way home from the hospital. For three months, regardless of time of day or night in a rural community that rolled up the sidewalks at 8:00 pm I had had to wait for traffic every time I got to it. In particular, one old man showed up almost every weekday driving his maximum speed of fifteen mph and leading a queue of at least fifteen cars. No matter what I did to my schedule, it seemed that he was always there when I got there and I had to wait for them all to go by so I could become "tail end Charlie"… once more! My way past that impasse lay in letting go of my anger over the situation… one of the most difficult challenges I ever had to meet. Furthermore, I had to release myself from the fear of not having the anger any more!

My ego knew something was wrong, but it could not see why it was always getting to that damn' stop sign just when traffic forced it to wait to join at the tail of the queue. That part of me which knew about limitless time and space—the soul that knew the old man's role in pointing me down the healing way—was collaborating with the old man's soul to bring us together, day after day. The student was ready, and it brought the teacher to me. Because the ego is finite, secular, and confined to the body, it cannot do such work. Only that which can go out of body and perceive patterns such as these can create such situations. Does it really happen with such regularity and ease? As my soul is always both "inside" and "outside," this is what comes naturally to it.

My ego continued to try to control situations that threatened it, especially when every few years I would do something quite incredibly stupid, and incur the wrath of someone close to me (p.39). However, it never succeeded. Success finally came when my soul led me to David Groves who took me back through the clam-digging trauma of my childhood (p.39). Once I had recovered this memory, I never again repeated that strange behavior. To this day, my ego has absolutely no idea of how I came to be on David Groves' mailing list! When he asks, "Why?" my soul shows him a knowing, peaceful smile.

Shortly after that healing experience, I received the invitation to take part in Elisabeth Kübler-Ross' deep-process[70] intensive at the Shaker village in southern Maine (p.13). In the ecstatic moment of watching the cemetery gate open all by itself I knew that I was in a deep, relationship with the Godhead. My soul had made sure my ego would misread the brochure and take the necessary steps to get me there where it would introduce me to the wonder of the Spirit.

That is how my midlife crisis ended.

Ego... and soul... and healing:

As I look back at the patterns of these events, the word, *coincidence*, comes to mind (p. 57). Popular definitions agree that the word describes occurrences which seem to have some connection and which *accidentally* happen at the same time. I sense the presence of a mystery in those words... a mystery I met through a H.O.P.E.'r who said, "Coincidences are only God's way of remaining anonymous." A friend rephrased it 15 years later, saying, "If you still believe in accidents, you simply haven't been paying attention."

Another friend calls these gentle and kind coincidences "grace notes." Once we give ourselves permission to recognize them, we find a certain grace manifesting itself every day in our lives. There seems to be a fine grace that touches and moves little things like mailing lists for workshops and intensives. There is a larger, more obvious, grace moving larger things, like latched garden gates. An even larger and more obvious grace protects slave ships in threatening storms, and gives birth to earth-changing hymns like *Amazing Grace*. All forms of grace are the soul collaborating with God.

Seeing grace in all things is a soul function. It is healing work—the work of becoming whole. H.O.P.E. work is soul work, as the words, "Healing Of Persons Exceptional" imply. It is the work of relationship—the sharing way. Healing is impossible in a separated, fearful ego-state, but it can begin through an intellectual effort of the ego that eventually leads to the soul's passion and compassion. The soul, the *relator* bringing us together, is responsible for all healing.

As anyone's memory grows, it becomes more complex and so do the ego's responses to the (immediate) physical and social world and its actions in that world. As complexity increases, the ego perceives that life is becoming fragmented—wounded—and it seeks, often frantically, to control this apparent disintegration. Without a spiritual source of support, its struggles can only increase in the face of what it sees is a curse.

The phrase, "in our wounded-ness our human-ness lies," speaks directly to the most powerful gift of life—that woundedness. Only the soul can see the gift in that which leads us to the valley of the shadow of death. There, the soul will work on it. There it will ask the ego to help with its resources of personality. There, the ego will agree to work so close to death, its arch-enemy, because the soul will help with its strength of spirit.

Would it not be easier on the ego if it knew what the soul knew? What if the master of the "what" of life and the master of the "who" of life were to come together in the "marriage of true minds" of Shakespeare's sonnet? Would we not conceivably discover "why" The Godhead gave us life and "how" we are to live? Would we not be "coming home"?

Homecoming

The ego and the soul work in the same domain—the body, our *ship of life*. To review my earlier comparison of the two, the ego is impulsive and the soul is subtle and shy. When the noisy ego recognizes the quiet soul's presence and agrees to collaborate with it, we truly have our ship on course, directed by a crew, not just one individual.

In "primitive" societies that recognize the presence of the soul, this integration of the ego and the soul takes place comfortably and progressively, nurtured from womb-time on through all stages of growth and development. At birth, the soul opens its wings to have a look around and see where it is. It folds its wings and waits while the newborn develops its physical and emotional senses over the next five years. It then opens its wings, looks around, and gives its soul cry, which the elders recognize and acknowledge. It shuts its wings again while the ego with which it is to work goes about developing *its* strengths, supported by those who know its passion. When the young one reaches puberty, the wings fly open and stay open. The Elders encourage the new, young adult to sing its soul-song, to dance its soul-dance, to cry its soul-cry. Having discovered the source of its nurturance, the young adult will mature beyond the waning strengths of the ego and give birth to a human being with a wisdom focus on service—serving The Creator by serving humanity with the highest good in mind.

When the ego first hearkens to the clarion song of the soul, it may pull back in confusion. However, the soul can reassure the ego and call it back to listen to the soul's alluring song and cry and to witness its beautiful dance. The soul, coming from a place of pure love, calls to the ego to join it in life. When the ego commits itself to dance and sing with the soul, their human home becomes a whole self... and s-he heals.

When we make this commitment, we stop trying to shape the soul to the ego's temporal and secular perceptions of reality. Instead, we encourage the ego to accept the soul's eternal and sacred image of that reality and surrender into the soul's embrace. This surrender is a journey of homecoming—a spiritual return that begins as soon as we realize the sacred wonder of each finite, individual life.

The soul knows that *its* journey is an inner, personal journey without measure. It knows that the body has lived a unique story. It knows that the ego is essential to its journey through eternity. The ego would like to believe what the soul knows, but its need to be separate holds it back. When the soul guides the ego through crisis, and the ego hears the lovely soul-cry, its old belief system falls apart. When the ego hears the soul acknowledge it for its strengths of form, talent, and temperament that helped it skillfully navigate the ocean of life, the ego now *believes* what the soul *knows*.

When the ego discovers that it is essential to the soul's journey, it agrees to a partnership with the soul, and healing accelerates. The soul, never sleeping, now holds the ego in its loving hands and lets the ego get the rest it needs. The partnership heals the life... the person *comes home* to the Self.

This concept of Homecoming developed smoothly and steadily from studying the psychology of success that I began in 1975, and from applying what I learned to hundreds of clinical situations in which I helped patients find meaning and value— hope—in their lives. The people I met in these situations have all blessed my life by sharing their personal experiences with me. I share their gifts with you.

This psychology has helped me greatly to understand and appreciate the struggles we go through in our lives. It has helped me immensely in my surgical career. It was the foundation of H.O.P.E., Healing Of Persons Exceptional in 1987 as a system of attitudinal healing support groups that acknowledge our humanness and honor our individuality.

This practical psychology aligns with the experience and teachings of Viktor Frankl, MD, the Austrian psychiatrist who found the meaning of life in four years' suffering in Nazi concentration camps.[71] While he was incarcerated, he finished the work he had begun over a decade earlier in Vienna titled *Die Ärtzliche Seelsorge*, later published in English as, *The Doctor and The Soul*. In the camps, he used his wonderful mind to develop a clever shorthand with which he kept track of his ideas on tiny pieces of paper. He maintained a passionate devotion to publishing the work that kept him alive through three years of hell from which only one in twenty-eight returned. After his liberation, and after regaining a significant part of his health, he quite literally launched that book and the now world-renowned *Man's Search for Meaning*[72]. He dictated the book to a team of three stenographer-typists who worked in shifts to keep up with his furious outpourings. In this way, it took only a matter of a few days to complete it and several others he had kept in his mind during his captivity.

He called his work *Logotherapy*, which can be summarized as *the psychology of meaning*. Gordon Allport of Harvard, who wrote the preface to *Man's Search for Meaning*, pressured him into writing a "nutshell of logotherapy" as the second part of the book. It is wonderful that he did, for, in Frankl's own words, "each part strengthens and complements the other"[73]. Out of his experience, Frankl found that: "The last of the human freedoms is to choose one's attitude in a given set of circumstances; to choose one's way. It is this spiritual freedom that cannot be taken away that makes life meaningful and purposeful (Man's Search for Meaning)."

This psychology and its underlying philosophy have contributed much to the lives of many. It is a way of empowering people that is easy to learn and apply. Frankl based it on practical experiences of life as it is; not as some theory would have it be! It guides people to their own healing with the awareness that healing is an inner, personal process which people choose to do to and for themselves. It is not something done to them by others. Many people in and out of the healing professions know from experience that the greatest healing influence they can have on self and others comes through the attitudes in which they hold their relationship with those others. Not that many people, however, see this as spiritual work. Frankl did. I do.

A dear friend and sometime patient of mine, Larry Fournier, has given me permission to include his story here, for it is a wonderful example of crisis, ego development and soul awareness.

Larry's first crisis exploded on him at the age of ten months on the day after he had taken his first two steps alone. When he awoke that morning, he could not walk. The doctor was called, and made the incredible[74] diagnosis of "infantile paralysis" (as poliomyelitis was called in 1932). Larry was literally "wiped out" by the disease. It was years before he would walk with crutches. He had his first surgery to stabilize his spine when he was four. By 1971, when we first met in the convenience store he owned and operated with the capable assistance of his wife, he had had over forty operations and had spent years in hospitals because of the effects of the disease. He was also a low handicap golfer, in spite of his deformed, stick-like legs, and the fact that he had to drive his golf cart to within six feet of the ball, and nearly lie on his back to lay out his putts.

The only handicap he saw in himself was five golf strokes. He said to me, "Doc, this was all I ever knew, and I never had the words, "handicapped" or "disabled" in my mind. I knew I was different from my brother, but I never let that bother me, and it never bothered my family, either."

He went on to say that he loved athletics, and that while his brother was an excellent athlete, people who knew them both often said to Larry that if he had his brother's legs, he would be a champion golfer. Larry's usual reply was "If I had his legs, I probably wouldn't be at all interested in golf today. I took it up because it was a challenge." Larry has thrived on challenges, and he has used his Roman Catholic upbringing to call upon his God for help in meeting his challenges. He got an immediate answer the first time he asked....

His family took him to the shrine of Sainte Anne de Beaupré in Quebec when he was seven. He could not stand on his left leg without it buckling under him because the knee would not lock. He went to the altar and asked God to help him walk. He turned around, and, carrying his crutches "like two shotguns," walked all the way back to his pew near the entrance to the large shrine. He knew in that moment that he was spiritually connected to the Universe and that God was asking him to show handicapped people what they could do with their lives!

Larry has lived with that mission ever since. He lives a simple life of example that has enriched hundreds of other lives.

My own Homecoming:

Several years ago, as I was becoming more aware of my ego as a *function* of my self, I had a strange set of images come to me. On one particular day, I had made a simple mistake in something I was doing, and I heard my voice saying, "Stupid!" Immediately, I had an image of a slightly younger me standing close to my right side, leaning around in front of me, looking me in the eye, and with an admonishing finger-shake, saying, "You know better than that!"

This was a brand-new experience! I had often admonished myself verbally for my mistakes, but I had never before had this visual image. It seemed as though I was standing at some sort of a workplace like a desktop with a computer on it, and I knew instantly that this other "me" was my ego. He was out of breath and looked a bit disheveled. I asked him where he had come from, to which he replied, "Out there," pointing to my right. I could see an open sliding glass door with a couple of steps going down to a lawn with a rather well worn path in the grass leading off to the left.

I said, "You stay out there, don't you?" to which he nodded in assent. Something distracted me then, and the image faded.

However, I kept coming back to this imaginary place with every stupid mistake. Once, as I looked out at the lawn and the well-worn path, I felt compelled to make his life easier. I saw that if I built a deck just outside those doors, and furnished it to his comfort; he would not have to run so far. When I made him the offer, he looked at me happily and said that would be great, and could he please have a chaise longue and a TV with a VCR so he could watch NASCAR races. I agreed, and in the instant it takes to create a mental image, the deck materialized, complete with railing, steps down to the lawn, and his furnishings. I put my arm around his shoulders, thanked him for his help, and suggested he go out there and relax. As we were walking out to the chaise longue, I asked if he would like a beer, offering him one of my favorites, to which he commented, "How'd you know? That's my favorite, too!"

He was a lot happier not having to run so far to make sure I was doing everything to his satisfaction. I also became happier, listening lovingly and quietly when he came in to set me straight with another of his lectures on the right way to do things. When he would finish his lecture, I would get up, put my arm around his shoulders and offer him a cold glass of his favorite beer and a Swiss cheese and Lebanon bologna sandwich—another favorite of ours. Then I might offer to put on the videotape of the latest NASCAR race that he missed because he was off white water canoeing on Maine's Carrabassett River. He often told me how great it was to have this time off after all these years of hard work.

A new relationship with my ego had begun. There was a shared space in my heart that was growing ever larger.

My life was now easier, and it was still as challenging as ever with my H.O.P.E. work. When cold weather came, we put an insulated sub-floor on the deck and enclosed it with double-paned glass windows. We hooked up to the heating system of my home, and put up window quilts for the bitter cold days. I traded in the old TV for a twenty-seven inch flat screen TV and bought a lighted end table with a shelf for his favorite reading material. I got him a small fridge of his own that I stocked with a choice of beers (by now I had a list of his favorites—all the same as mine, by the way) and some of his favorite foods.

This process of caring for my ego went on for more than a year. During that time, the rest of the house, of which this deck and the kitchen-dining area were a part, took shape in my mind. The workstation to which I referred was central, facing the south[75]. My ego's sliding doors and deck were on the west side, opening onto a wide lawn bordered by woods. The front door faced the east with a gravel walk to the edge of the road, where there was a mailbox next to a gate in a white rail fence. The kitchen-dining area was in the southeast corner. Behind me on the north side of my house was a large, open, space with a warm brick fireplace in the east wall, and a comfortable leather reclining chair facing it. There were shelves of books and a good sound system with its own stacks of favorite records, tapes, and CDs. This was my home, but I still could not see where my ego lived.

Over time, I became aware that the southwest corner to the left of the deck that I built for my ego was a featureless, gray-walled space. It remained that way until late in 1998; I was telling a H.O.P.E. group about this house of mine, and my ego walked quietly in through his door saying, "C'mere, I wanna show you something." I immediately began telling the group what I was hearing inside my mind.

"Okay," I said, putting down my pen, and we walked out onto the deck. The gray, featureless wall to the left had changed. It was now white-clapboarded like the rest of the house, and in its center was an open door!

"Go on in," he said. I walked into a cheery bathroom in bright colors with a curtained window facing west. "Mine," he said, adding, "Go on through."

There was another door in the opposite wall leading into a yellow bedroom-study with windows on the south and west walls. There was an outside door in the south wall next to the window. A door in the east wall led into the kitchen-dining area. (Now I knew why I had difficulty keeping the kitchen fridge fully stocked!) There were cupboards and cabinets arranged on all of the walls of the room. All had locks, most of which were open. The few that were still locked looked like they had not been disturbed for a long time.

"I thought you'd like to see where I live," he said. "I've opened a whole lot of locked spaces over last few years, but not all of them."

"Are you going to open them, too?" I asked.

"Some day, when you're ready," he replied.

"How will you know?"

"I get ideas from somewhere that I know I gotta listen to, that's how. When I do open up something I thought I'd locked away for good, it always seems like the right thing to do," he said.

"How do you know that?" I asked.

"I know that because it *feels good*!" came the answer.

I told him how grateful I was that he had shown me where he had lived all this time. He put a hand on my arm, and grinned in silence... he did not have to say a thing. I told him I had something to show him. We went back to my workstation, where I opened a drawer and took out a framed quote from Sam Walter Foss (1858 - 1911) that said, "Let me live in a house by the side of the road and be a friend to man."[76] Together, smiling, and with tears in our eyes, we hung it up on the wall in front of my workplace.

I am more whole now than at any time since the summer of 1937. I know with striking clarity that I made my homecoming possible because I put my arm around my ego's shoulders and he knew in that moment that I loved him. The home we have found in my heart is our home. We make a heck of a team.

He is aware that his work is nearly done. Soon, he will open the few remaining locked places in his room, and he will let me assimilate him completely. We will keep his name, Ken, which is Old English for *I know*. This can only happen when I love him completely and perfectly. Where I once tried to banish him, he hid in that featureless corner of my house; now I welcome him and love him. I do not ever want him to hide again.

I admit there are times that I wished he would stop being so stubborn and persistent, but he has always been a part of me, and now we honor and love each other for the work we have done together. These days, he spends most of his time in the kitchen or on that lovely deck, keeping an eye on me. He has his own sound system now with the country-western music he has loved since childhood. He has a good science fiction library and many videotapes of NASCAR races and kayak water sports. He has his own computer with games and Internet hook-ups. He is a happy camper... and so am I.

You, too, are both a soul and an ego. How would you like to come Home?

Part 2: Circling *Your* Soul

Witnessing...

You are a one-of-a-kind work of art;
Display it...

You are a once told tale;
Tell it...

You are a once sung song;
Sing it...

You are a once read poem;
Read it...

You are a once danced dance;
Dance it...

You have shown me the wonder of your soul.

You honor me. Thank you

Coming home is a journey of continual returns... a spiral journey that circles back to familiar people, places, and things... always in a new perspective. To tell your story of return is to circle your soul.

As the first part of SoulCircling lay in the spiritual nature of H.O.P.E. Groups, I invite you to read what I have written about their structure and function, for it is in H.O.P.E. Groups that people found meaning in their lives. For many, the discovery was a spiritual one—a discovery of their True (or Higher) Self. When people found their Self in a H.O.P.E. Group, the physical/ mental/emotional condition that first brought them to the group took second place to their *life*. The principles implied in the reading of the "Golden Book" at the beginning of each H.O.P.E. Group meeting contain the wisdom of the ages, and set the tone for this profound personal change.

The exercises that follow in the chapter on SoulCircling grew out of the H.O.P.E. Group work and my interaction with a wonderful group of people who called themselves The Nurturers, all of whom are named in the acknowledgments. These exercises will guide you to a point at which you can hear your soul-song and witness its beauty-dance. Having reached this point in your life, you have discovered fire once again, the passionate soul fire that cleanses and purifies, exposing that core of Universal love that holds everything in perfect relationship.

You will learn to work with others in a small group that uses synergy to help you clarify our soul's intention—to discover what you came here to do. Here, you will discover the power of listening, so that you may ask questions for personal clarification only. You will listen with your heart. You will learn to *reflect* and *affirm* rather than to suggest, recommend, judge, or criticize. You will reflect out of your listening. You will learn the power of affirmation and you will share it with each other.

SoulCircling helps you walk your talk and talk your walk; they become *congruent*. Be congruent and you make your life and its messages *coherent*; the world will respect you for this, even though some will fear you. You will be called honest, which some groups recognize as the single symptom of recovery from any addiction. Honesty invites the return of *integrity*. Integrity implies wholeness and wholeness is identical to health. A small group that follows these principles is a safe group, a nurturing group, a loving group, and a healing group. Such a group is a *SoulCircle.*

In a SoulCircle, you can take a fearless, loving inventory of the resources with which you meet life—those assets that comprise valuable elements of your personality: your physical form, talents, temperament, will, and passion. You will identify and acknowledge your responsibilities and attachments to people, places and things. You will add them to the story of how you became what you are today, and they become an invaluable resource for recognizing your soul's journey in this lifetime. Describe yourself in these terms to your SoulCircle. It will help you shape an intention for your life and an empowering affirmation of it. Now you have truly begun to circle your soul—you are coming Home.

Chapter 6: H.O.P.E., Healing Of Persons Exceptional

Principle:

- Support groups that focus on intention nurture healing and wholeness.

Meeting the needs of the ego and the soul:

In Chapter Five, we brought together in a *homecoming* the most vital aspects of self, ego and soul,. Now that they are both in the House by the Side of the Road, they need to keep up the dialogue they began while the ego still secluded itself in its private quarters. Ego needs to talk about its worries and concerns and soul needs to talk about its passion. They need to add another chair to the great room on the north side of their house and sit in safety and intimacy while they figure out the ways to get the soul work done.

Ego wants to be safe, as any ego wants to be safe, so that it can talk about itself. It is accustomed to judging and being judged, both of which cause it to retreat behind familiar boundaries. It wants to complain about the painful things that happened to it and boast about its accomplishments. It wants to love and be loved. It is familiar with criticism, having given and received it all of its life; it has found acceptance in the embrace of its Friend. It is accustomed to giving and receiving advice. Now it needs none, having committed itself to its Friend's knowledge and experience. It simply needs to be heard.

Soul wants safety, too, as any butterfly-like creature would. It wants to have space in which to spread its wings and show its beauty. It does not like cages, and yet it will submit to being caught in a gentle web of gossamer by one who loves it and who agrees to serve it. It remembers that the one who loves it always lets it go—free to fly wherever it wants—knowing that it will return in its own time. It needs to be reassured that its wings will not be pinned down under the scrutiny of someone who would analyze and dissect it to find out how it is made and of what it is made. It, too, needs to know that it is loved, for love gives it joy.

Whereas the ego has extensive experience with judgment (and reasoned, analytic thought to support its judgment), the soul benefits not from any analysis, but from the love that nurtures it and promotes its growth. Indeed, the soul and its passions are parts of the Universal Mystery that may forever defy scientific analysis and yet forever remain available to human experience. Both the ego and the soul need a safe place in which to talk about their needs, desires, and passions.

The Story of H.O.P.E.

In 1987, I created a support group in my surgical practice to help people with cancer find meaning in their lives. Here is the story of how the 501(c)(3) H.O.P.E. organization grew out of my experience with helping these wonderful people with cancer find meaning and value in their lives.

In 1975, I began to familiarize myself with Earl Nightingale's lifelong study of the essence of success (p. 11). Nightingale was responsible for showing me that our *attitude* was the key to accessing these resources because they determine the way in which we direct our minds. History had shown him that when people took control of their attitudes, they took control of their lives. When I started helping my patients take charge of *their* attitudes, their lives changed for the better, as had mine. This supported my personal growth and development. I supported theirs, in turn, and so goes the cycle of the Law of Returns (p. 11).

In 1985 because of the major life impacts of this work, I began to study psychology under the direction of the gifted psychiatrist, Barry Wood (p. 12), MD, through whom I met Bernie Siegel, MD and Jerry Jampolsky, MD. Barry is gone, though he remains in spirit, and both Bernie and Jerry are friends and advisors to H.O.P.E. and me to this day.

H.O.P.E. Groups

At the first group meeting, the group decided it wanted to continue, and to call themselves a H.O.P.E. Group. I challenged them to find the words to fit the acronym. At the next meeting, the nurse who had encouraged me to start the group, Sharon Williams, RN, offered "Healing Of Persons Exceptional," and got cheers for her idea. Each word came to have specific meaning. *Healing,* meant to become whole, without any implication that one had to be *cured of her or his disease* in order to heal. (Traditionally, humans are of four parts, body, mind, soul, and spirit. To heal is to bring those together into one—to integrate oneself.) *Persons* spoke to our common humanness—our *oneness.* (The Eastern spiritual traditions of Hinduism, Buddhism, and Taoism focus on this particular quality of being human.) On the other hand, the Western spiritual traditions of Judaism, Christianity, and Islam focused on our *uniqueness,* that which makes us all *Exceptional.* In H.O.P.E., we chose to focus on *both* our oneness and our uniqueness. In this way, we found we could direct our thoughts away from tendencies of the ego to focus on uniqueness as *specialness* and *exclusiveness* and redirect them toward the inclusive way of *oneness* and *uniqueness* that is the function of the soul.

A H.O.P.E. group is a relationship-centered group. The relationships are loving, caring and compassionate—attitudes that direct the growth of group. They lead to the awareness that a H.O.P.E. group is a "safe place" where people can safely tell their stories and sincerely listen to others'; where they can talk about and validate feelings; where they can develop their power to live and discover their full range of resources for living. Their relationships, couched in loving, compassionate attitudes, effect those changes. They learn to focus on hope, the attitude of possibility, meaning, value, and purpose. They do not deny what might be "wrong", but appreciate the *lesson* to be learned therefrom and reframe the wrong into something that works right. They do not focus on problems, for they know that only keeps them in the problem. They focus on possibilities, for they know that will help them rise above and go beyond the problem. Indeed, H.O.P.E. is an "MVP" program—one that helps people find Meaning, Value, and Purpose in their lives.

The attitude of the relationships in a H.O.P.E. Group is love, unconditional love. Participants are not there to change others, only themselves. Love provides the stable platform, the safe place, the compassion, and the support for everyone in a H.O.P.E. Group.

An important semantic difference about a H.O.P.E. Group is the focus contained in its name, namely, *hope* and *healing*. H.O.P.E. Groups are not cancer support groups, AIDS support groups, or depression support groups, *because they do not support those conditions*. Rather, as noted, they acknowledge the conditions and at the same time, they encourage detaching from them and focusing on life. There are H.O.P.E. Groups for people with cancer, but the focus is on hope and healing. The same is true for H.O.P.E. Groups for people with AIDS, or depression, or anxiety, or any of the other critical physical and mental that can affect human beings. Our experience shows us that no category of individual must be excluded from a H.O.P.E. Group. Our experience also shows us that there are some categories of illness that make participation in such groups difficult, especially schizophrenic conditions, multiple personality disorders, sociopathic and psychopathic personalities.

This context of group work is not as common as one might wish. A man who had been crippled by polio when he was seven said, "I've been in groups all over the Northeast, and have never been anything like a H.O.P.E. Group... it's the only place I want to be!"

The years that have passed since the first H.O.P.E. group came together have shown the continued effectiveness of H.O.P.E. and its programs that now include training people in the H.O.P.E. cognitive restructuring process, and the experiential workshops, *Circling the Soul: Coming Home to Yourself*®, and *The Art and Soul of Healing*. Some trainees and workshop participants are interested in guiding groups, and the center helps them start these groups. My over twenty years experience in this particular form of cognitive restructuring makes it possible to provide ongoing support for those whom we have trained and their groups.

Since its beginning, H.O.P.E. has grown from one group of people challenged by cancer to many groups of people experiencing a wide range of challenges, including cancer, diabetes, chronic hepatitis, autoimmune diseases, multiple sclerosis, chronic fatigue syndrome (CFIDS), reflex sympathetic dystrophy (RSDS), bereavement, recovery from alcoholism, depression, anxiety, trauma, and loss of self-esteem. We have added the two workshops to provide reasonably healthy people with a short, intense experience of the H.O.P.E. process, and to provide health care professionals with an effective means of *nurturing* their patients and clients in the time constraints in which we find ourselves as we move further into the millennium.

In all our work we encourage and teach people to focus on what they would like to have happen in their lives, rather than what is wrong with those lives. We introduce people to attitudes that have helped thousands of others throughout the ages. In this way, *their problems become the keys to their growth* We are not so much interested in what caused any problem as in the attitudes and beliefs that help get past it. When H.O.P.E.'rs do this work, they get clear on the meaning in their lives. They feel better and become healthier.

H.O.P.E. groups are open and ongoing. They are always confidential. Caring people who are doing their own healing work guide them. These fine persons have been trained in the H.O.P.E. process, and meet as needed as a group with a senior guide to share their experiences. H.O.P.E. "guides" are not supposed to "fix" or "treat" others. If a person in their group needs "therapy", the guide encourages the person to seek that professional help.

H.O.P.E. does not charge any fees to participate in a H.O.P.E. group. H.O.P.E. is a volunteer, non-profit organization, and it does accept contributions to help with its outreach and growth. We believe that people like to make contributions that acknowledge the value of what they have received. In this way, a group has the right to choose to support its guide and their meeting place with their contributions. H.O.P.E. supports the work of its guides with ongoing trainings and open lines of communication. H.O.P.E. encourages its group members to support their guides in ways that acknowledge their time spent with the group, their out-of-pocket expenses, and their willingness to study and learn more about the process.

It does not take a special degree to guide a H.O.P.E. Group. We have trained school teachers, nurses, fishermen, and house-wives to guide these groups. People who do personal *coaching* tend to make excellent H.O.P.E. Group guides.

The style of a H.O.P.E. group:

H.O.P.E. Groups all have the following in common:
- a specific mental structure with which they open the meeting—*the crucible*
- confidentiality
- openness—the agenda walks in through the door, and no one is ever late
- focus on healing and wellness
- support for the processes of each individual's life
- affirmation of its members' stories and intentions
- showing neither judgment nor criticism but uncondi-tional love

The crucible of a H.O.P.E. Group meeting:

H.O.P.E. Groups set the context of each meeting (the content walks in through the door) by taking turns, one phrase at a time, reading the following:

The H.O.P.E. Group opening:

We are a H.O.P.E. group.
We come together to find wellness.

Wellness comes with the discovery of peace of mind.
We find peace of mind through understanding and letting go of
guilt and fear.
In this way, we learn to live in each moment.
In this moment, we can choose to focus on the whole of life
rather than its fragments.
We seek the power that makes this choice possible.
We come to realize that this power lies within each one of us.
This power, as we understand it, is Love.
With Love's power we come to realize the promise of Hope.

The Principles of Attitudinal Healing:

(With deep gratitude to Jerry Jampolsky and the Centers for
Attitudinal Healing, worldwide.)

The essence of our being is love.
Health is inner peace. Healing is letting go of fear.
Giving and receiving are the same.
We can let go of the past and of the future.
Now is the only time there is and each instant is for giving.
We can learn to love ourselves and others by forgiving rather
than judging.
We can become love finders rather than fault finders.
We can choose and direct ourselves to be peaceful inside re-
gardless of what is happening outside.
We are students and teachers to each other.
We can focus on the whole of life rather than the fragments.
Since love is eternal, death need not be viewed as fearful.
We can always perceive others as either extending love or call-
ing for help.

The H.O.P.E. group guidelines:

We agree to:

1) help the group focus on attitudinal healing by letting go of fear and conflict, and seeing life in a peaceful and loving way.
2) work on our own healing processes, offer mutual support and practice non-judgmental listening.
3) recognize the importance of each person's process, and in this way we create a safe atmosphere for the whole group.
4) support each other's inner guidance, and to trust in that process.
5) share what has worked for us in our own lives without expectation of it working for others; for there are no "shoulds".
6) risk and expose our own emotional states, and thus we share our common experience.
7) use our time together with mutual care, consideration and respect.
8) be students and teachers to each other... interchangeably.
9) maintain a loving focus on each speaker, and refrain from cross-talk or walking on another's talk.
10) keep all personal information that is shared in a H.O.P.E. meeting strictly confidential.

Filling the crucible:

We have learned that the agenda for each meeting walks in through the door. We introduce ourselves to newcomers and often ask them how they found their way to this H.O.P.E. Group meeting. We then share with them how we found our way to it, and why we keep coming back. (Sometimes the two questions have different answers.) We follow the guidelines to help us keep on track. They are flexible, as individual needs dictate, for some people occasionally need a lot of time to talk about all that has happened. The guide sees to it that everyone is acknowledged with an opportunity to speak.

Closing the H.O.P.E. Group meeting:

We use the "Prayer for Serenity" (sometimes slightly modified to suit the sentiments of the group):

> God (Love), grant us the serenity
> To accept the things we cannot change,
> The courage to change the things we can,
> And the wisdom to know the difference.

Finally:

If you would like more information about attending or guiding groups, or the H.O.P.E. process, please contact us at H.O.P.E. Go to our web site; it will show you how we can do the introduction and training over the Internet. We would be pleased to send you more information, including our episodic-periodic newsletter, *Ripples*.

You are invited to contact the author at:

P.O. Box 276
52 High Street
South Paris, ME 04281-0276

tel. (207) 743-7458 (M, F between 10:30 and 11:00 a.m. and M, W, F between 2:00 and 2:30 p.m.

email: kenhhope@hopehealing.org (24/7)

Visit our web sites: www.hopehealing.org, www.soulcircling.com, www.hopelifecoach.com

Chapter 7: SoulCircles

Principles:

- In the last chapter, we saw how a H.O.P.E. Group helps people discover the soul's purpose and bring meaning to their lives.
- Whereas a H.O.P.E. Group does the work in short meetings over a long time, a SoulCircle[77] provides a safe place for the work to be done in less than two days.

Small groups:

SoulCircles, as I use them in my work, are *small groups* that convene for the express purpose of helping one, some, or all of its members open the envelope(s) that contains their "Earth Orders." A SoulCircle can be of any size. It may consist of none other than your self—your soul and your ego—and this book. It helps to have The Friend for company, but you may not want It at this time. The intimate company of a small group of up to five or six familiar, caring friends in addition to this book comprises an ideal SoulCircle. Intimacy evolves from our innermost nature, our *essence*, and asks that we open our hearts to each other. It creates those safe relationships that become the crucible of synergistic[78] minds.

SoulCircles have a precedent in Quaker clearness committees. Quakers, members of The Religious Society of Friends, have successfully used clearness committees for over three hundred years to conduct the pastoral affairs of their meetings. I have come to appreciate the power of clearness committees through a lifetime of exposure to Quaker ways. My experience with Quaker ways began with childhood readings, developed out of a Quaker college experience, and matured through my adult studies and practices. I appreciate clearness committees for their ability to do creative, supportive work without the direction of a trained minister, counselor, or "facilitator."

In Quaker practice, a Friend[79] seeking help in finding a solution to a problem (a *concern* in Quaker terminology) convenes a clearness committee to which s-he brings the concern[80]. As s-he is (obviously) the center of attention for the clearness committee, s-he is its *focus person*—and they are her or his *support persons.* Friends make wonderful support persons because of their support and sympathy.

However, their supportive, sympathetic *personalities* can interfere with the conduct of the clearness committee. Quakers long ago established guidelines that would help support people avoid personality traps when they worked in clearness committees. Because Quakers believe that the "light of God" is within everyone, the focus person has within her or him all of the resources s-he needs in order to resolve her or his concern. Therefore, the support persons who comprise the committee do not have to judge, criticize, make recommendations, or give advice. Instead, they *ask open, honest questions* for personal clarification only; they *reflect* on what the focus person is saying and share those reflections; and they *affirm* the focus person for her or his work on the concern.

These guidelines take a tremendous ego burden off the shoulders of the members of the committee—the members do not have to fix or change anything. It is up to the focus person to effect those changes that came up in the meeting(s). It should be clear to the reader that everyone on the committee is expected to ask his or her ego to be silent while the soul asks the questions, reflects on the associations, and affirms the focus person. Quaker-Rumi ways of doing the work with the unseen presence of The Friend facilitates the process.

The Quaker educator, Parker J. Palmer, led me and twenty-four previously unacquainted people through a workshop experience of the value and power of clearness committees. He asked for five people to volunteer as focus persons and randomly chose the four support people for each of them. Within a matter of two hours, we completed the work to the satisfaction and benefit of each focus person.

SoulCircling was already using small group process and experiencing its wonderful benefits. The addition of the clearness committee guidelines added a powerfully supportive quality to the process. SoulCircles use these principles of Quaker clearness committees without any pretense of trying to be a copy of any religion. However, the work is clearly spiritual, and its spiritual nature addresses the fundamental questions of life without any religious bias. SoulCircles and SoulCircling are suitable for participants of all spiritual callings including scientism and atheism[81].

Participants in SoulCircling workshops describe the process as one of taking a fearless personal inventory of their assets and describing them to like-minded, supportive people. They find that this process of self-revelation shows them ways to release themselves of their attachments to people, places, and things that have owned them and taken their power away throughout their lifetimes—people, places, and things that rent space in their minds. Through this exquisitely loving process, participants free themselves from their fear, anger, and hatred and become compassionately accepting of the people to whom they were attached—the basis of all true forgiveness. The consequence is individual freedom and the recovery of personal power.

For those who come to SoulCircling occasions sponsored by H.O.P.E., we have developed the following guidelines that we read aloud together at the beginning of the SoulCircle work.

> We are a SoulCircle.
>
> We come together in support of each other.
>
> We agree to hold each other in loving regard and respect at all times.
>
> We agree to withhold all criticism and suspend all judgment.

> We agree to refrain from all tendencies to give advice
> or make recommendations.

> We agree to listen with heart and mind and reflect fairly
> and honestly on that which we see and hear.

> We agree to affirm each focus person for her or his
> unique gifts.

> We agree to keep all personal information shared in this
> SoulCircle in complete confidence.

For those who would do this work on their own, I recommend they print out the guidelines, give a copy of them to each support person, and read them together, out loud, at the beginning of the SoulCircling process.

This is obviously a verbal contract. Quakers do their business with verbal contracts saving written ones for egos that work in the absence of The Friend. In reading the guidelines out loud, every support person has given her or his *word* that s-he will support the entire meeting in the ways they have just expressed!

Because the purpose of a SoulCircle is to help the focus person find out the purpose of her or his soul's journey on Earth in this lifetime, their usual concern is along the lines of, "How do I find the meaning, value, and purpose of my life?" Our SoulCircle response to that question is, "Tell us your story. Take a fearless inventory of your assets of form and spirit and share it with us. Tell us what you would advise a person with that experience and those assets to do with her or his life that can be of greatest benefit to self, others, and The Friend. Lastly, let us affirm you for your good work."

SoulCircles have a lot in common with other small groups such as sewing circles, quilting circles, or craft circles. Their purpose is simply to *support* their members while they do something in common. SoulCircles search for those paths of life that bring meaning to the lives of all their participants. The work of circling one's soul is never done, so SoulCircles can continue to meet for a lifetime.

Love is the primary characteristic of a SoulCircle. Love is the essence of open and honest relationships. It is the source of the compassion that underlies all forgiveness. It is the context[82] in which we work. It is critical to the successful achievement of SoulCircling process. Love empowers the group to take responsibility for holding non-judgmental thoughts and offering kind words to each other.

Hope is a secondary characteristic of a SoulCircle. It is the attitude of meaning and possibility.

Intention is the focus of a SoulCircle, for it focuses on discovering the reason for a soul to come into human form.

Faith is the belief system behind the spiritual process of a SoulCircle.

The ancient and fundamental *Law of Returns* (p. 11)stands behind the function of a SoulCircle. Our actions affect many others, especially those close to us. Remember, when I complained to my friend that the world seemed to be angry with me, I found out that the world was responding to my prevailing attitude, so give the focus person what you would like to get when your turn comes.

The purpose of the group is not to understand the focus person, for to "stand under" a person is only to take the measure of that person's size and weight. It only defines her or him with physical dimensions. Understanding can be as blind as Atlas stooped over bearing the weight of the world on his mighty shoulders, not knowing what he carries except that it is heavy, large, and round. In the spiritual realm, the physical dimensions do not matter; what does matter is the dimension of the soul, which in reality cannot be measured in time or space. Accordingly, there can be no limit to its potential.

The group's primary responsibility is to support the focus person by keeping in mind the awareness that the focus person has all the answers within. "Feedback" is a living instrument affirming the focus person by answering the question, "How am I doing?" It draws her attention to what she has said and done, encouraging and supporting her change and growth. It allows her to create her own self-evaluation.

Feedback is a part of all living things. We cannot live for long without it. We grow with it from the time we are conceived! Angry, fearful feedback is inappropriate and harmful. We need loving feedback, which holds us in respect and care. Feedback is not instruction. It is Nature and Spirit talking to us... body and soul working together. When we choose to pay attention to how they work together, we learn as much about harmony as we do about discord.

SoulCircle support persons take notes that will help them recall the points of the story that got their attention. They take note of subtle changes in voice or posture and what seemed to bring them on. They leave analysis and understanding out of their thoughts by listening with their heart. The notes are for the benefit of the focus person, so they need to embrace the storyteller and the story in compassion that doubles her or his joy and halves her or his suffering. They help support persons reflect on what they saw and heard and affirm the focus person for her or his wealth of spirit. Later, they will jog the focus person's memory for details s-he did not see immediately. Support persons make a gift of these written notes to the focus person.

Support persons are there for but one person, the focus person. When their individual time comes to assume that role, they will find the others there for them—what goes 'round, comes 'round.

It usually takes less than an hour for the focus person to make his presentation to SoulCircle and to receive this kind of nurturing support from them. Every member of the group benefits from the work whether or not s-he takes a turn as the focus person. In SoulCircling workshops, people who have been through the process commonly come to other SoulCircling workshops to guide those who are inexperienced. Though they do not take a turn as focus person, they routinely feel enriched by this new experience.

Our experience with SoulCircling workshops has shown us that a SoulCircle of four or five people provides enough support to develop synergy, and yet is small enough to be able to get the work done in a reasonable length of time. We have learned to encourage workshop participants to convene their *own* SoulCircles in a month or six weeks to help them review what they have done. The group can be their friends, members of their congregation, participants from their SoulCircling workshop or from other guided groups that gather for creating synergy for each other. With these principles, it is relatively easy to learn how to come together in this kind of a group. The information and exercises of this book make it possible for other members of such a newly formed SoulCircle to help each other through the same process.

You are now ready for the creative work of your SoulCircle—SoulCircling.

Chapter 8: SoulCircling

Principle:

- You can create your own SoulCircle and set the gossamer web in which you will catch your soul and ask it what it came here to do.

Preparation:

First, you must set the environment in which that butterfly, Psyche, can allow itself to be held in the loving hearts and help you develop the four elements of SoulCircling: your StoryCircle, your Inventory, your Intention, and your Affirmation.

Butterflies like warmth, light, water, and food. A gossamer web stretched across a sled dog trail in Alaska in the middle of winter is not likely to catch a butterfly, but the environment of a SoulCircle provides everything you might need for butterfly-catching over the course of a few hours.

Second, You will need the following materials: a sheet or two of 8½ by 11 paper for notes, two large sheets of easel paper that you can get from your school or library, and some colored pencils or pens.

Third, if you do this with only this book for company, provide for your own comfort. If you convene a small group of friends, provide for their comfort, too. If you have engaged the services of a H.O.P.E. LifeCoach[83], go through your checklist and see that everything is ready for your talk with her or him.

Let us take the four elements in order.

Your StoryCircle:

You are living a life unique in the annals of the universe. It is a single story in an encyclopedic collection of stories that comprise the journey of your soul. Your story—ugly and beautiful,

sweet and sour, joyful and sad, painful and comfortable, wounded and healed—is a once-told tale of Universal value. It tells about your creativity. It tells about how you got strong in broken places. It is essential to understanding where you are going. It is a pleasure and an honor to hear you tell it. It is a delight to see your images of it. Yes, we want to see your story as well as hear it... and we do not expect you to be a visual artist.

Take one large sheet of easel paper and write "My Story" across the top. Take the other large sheet and write "My Intention" across the top of it. Put them aside.

Take a sheet of 8½ by 11 paper and write "My inventory" at the top. Set it aside for now. Take another sheet of 8½ by 11 paper and write "Life-shaping events" at the top. Now say to yourself, "What are those events that have shaped my life and brought me to this day?" Give yourself *two minutes* and, as quickly as possible, list those life-changing events as they come to mind. (The average adult will recall between eight and fifteen of them in those two minutes. Please do not dwell on them; today's important ones are right up front, ready to go on the paper.)

The list may not be in chronological order as you wrote them out, so number them now in the order in which they happened in your life.

Take the "My Story" sheet of easel paper and decide what kind of a background you would like for your Story. Perhaps the simplest of all is a circle, so we shall work with that as a starter[84]. Pencil in a faint circle almost as big as the sheet and put a mark at the top of the circle where the "12" would on be on a clock face. Midnight or noon, this is the point where dusk and dawn lie equally behind and before you. In SoulCircling, this point is midnight; for the next step, which is but a moment in time, takes you toward morning. How you take it sets the stage for how you meet the light of the coming day. Indeed, you are always at the morning of the rest of your life.

Please note: every successful person knows at the bottom of her or his heart that success comes from the way with which s-he meets the new day. Also, note this: success is, in and of itself,

not the goal; it is the *process* of moving *towards* the goal. What you are about to experience and create will help you choose the way in which you greet each new day—your attitude. Note midnight well, for it marks a truly remarkable event—the moment of your birth into the rest of your life. Note well the attitude with which you meet the day, for it will come back to you reflected by a million facets of your life. Remember, your attitude is <u>always</u> your choice.

Using midnight as the starting point, make a mark for each of the numbers in your list, spacing them fairly regularly around a clockwise circle. In the space you have chosen for the first event, draw a little picture of it. Draw a picture of the second event in the second space. Move around the circle this way until every space contains an image of a point in your story. Work on the background until it is complete in your eyes and mind. Take however much time as you need for this; it is important. Embellish your artwork with those colors and shapes that suit you.

This is your StoryCircle. It has never happened this way to anyone before you came to Earth and it will never happen to anyone after you leave. It can only happen in the space and time you have occupied, a space and time promised you from the beginning of Time, so it deserves to be expressed in whatever way is most important for you. This piece of art is as yet unfinished. Don't worry; you have all of the resources you need with which to complete it, as you shall see.

In the center of the StoryCircle, draw a container symbol in which you can write your favorite name for yourself. If you are like me, the name may not be the name your parents gave you. The name in the middle of my StoryCircle is "Rookie," to whom I introduced you earlier (p. 51). He appeared in my night dreams as often as he did in my daydreams. We were a racing team that owned a red racecar. Shortly after the "rescue" from the waters of Great Peconic Bay, I dreamt we died in a racing car crash. We did not die, though; we were above our bodies looking down at them with a remarkable sense of peace.

Rookie said, "I'm leaving you now."

"Will you be back?" I asked

"Someday," he said.

He came back fifty-two years later when I was participating in a guided visualization on forgiveness. We are one now, a team again, and I drew our racing car in the center of my circle and put our name on it.

Did you have an imaginary playmate when you were a child? Did a parent or grandparent have a special name for you that made you feel very good when she said it? This could be a soul-name; the associated image could be a soul-image. As you reflect on what I have just said, let your own soul-image come to mind, draw it in the center of the circle, and sign it with your soul name. Stand back, give yourself a hug, and say, "Welcome home!"

Your Inventory:

With the completion of the story circle, the next steps develop a loving inventory of your assets with which you make your soul's journey; assets your soul knew it would have when it incarnated. You will describe yourself—as a person—in this part of the exercise. You will also discover the *acres of diamonds*[85] on which you stand that give you the resources you need to complete your soul's work in this part of its journey. Let us examine the essentials of your inventory.

Now pick up the sheet of 8½ by 11 paper on which you have written the words "My inventory." It will be a list of your qualities that comprise each of the following:

- your genetic gifts of form, intelligence(s), talent(s), temperament;
- your soul's (archetypal) core passion;
- your attachments and responsibilities to people place and things (p. 57);
- your goals and intentions;
- your will;

Divide the sheet up into six equal parts, put the name of the quality in the top of each part, and, following the guidelines below, complete your inventory. (If you have difficulty with any part, get the help of your soul circle, your H.O.P.E. LifeCoach, or a friend or family member who knows you intimately and well.)

Your genetic gifts:

I first mentioned (p. 19) the genetic assets of form, intelligence, talents, and temperament, and I have referred to them several times since. In this exercise, you are going to describe them. Your soul knew it would share these with your ego. It knew the physical form it would occupy: female or male, tall or short, thick or thin, pale or dark, beautiful or plain. It knew the amount and kind of intelligence you would have. It knew that your body would harbor specific talents—*natural skills*. Talents are always those things that come especially easy ("Why can't *they* do it; it's so easy."). Everybody has them; they are precious to everybody, mothers and presidents alike, and often objects of scorn by jealous bullies. Your soul also knew that it would come to this world to experience life with a particular temperament with which you would respond to the varieties of people, places, and things that you would meet on your journey.

Your (archetypal) core passion:

I would remind you that all of the above characteristics have their origins in your genes. I would offer you that your ego most likely will feel sad, mad, or glad about those genetic influences because of its judgmental nature. At the same time, your soul accepts your genes without judgment, knowing that these genetic attributes are gifts that it works with to be able to follow its "Earth Orders" (p. 65). Whereas the engine of your ego's drive is survival, your soul's engine is its core passion that lights your fires and resonates deeply inside you. It is the object of your longing. It is what you love to do—what you would rather do than anything else—your soul's calling—and your Earth Orders direct you to follow it.

I would like to add here that the core passion can be identified with archetypal images from way back in human history, which further supports the idea of the transcendent nature of soul. In its most recent incarnations, your soul developed a passion to follow an *archetype*, an *original model of thought and behavior.* Archetypes come with identifying labels such as teacher, mechanic, nurse, doctor, lawyer, Indian chief, mother, father, actor, prophet, healer, or mason. Any time you say of someone, "Oh, she's a typical _____," you have just named an archetype. Its label has appeared, easy to read, right in front of your eyes. The ancient Greeks knew their archetypes well; they called them gods and goddesses[86]. They saw people as blends of these divine archetypes, and they were aware of the extreme danger for a human to follow a single archetype. Witness what happened to Norman Jean Baker when she became Marilyn Monroe and chose the way of Aphrodite, the goddess of love. As usually happens in such cases, history will keep our memories of her alive for a long, long time. She will still be alive long after our names become carvings on headstones.

Whether a person lives the life of one archetype or a blend of archetypes, s-he is still a one-of-a-kind work of art. Your soul has explored the challenges of becoming a *series* of such artworks with the talents of each of these archetypes. It knows that its archetypes always have different resources with which to work each time around. Your ego has likely given little consideration to this spiritual awareness, but SoulCircling draws one's ego into a new perception of its role and purpose. This part of the exercise can lead you to a greater appreciation of the archetypes you work with in this incarnation[87].

Your attachments and responsibilities:

Your ego, with its memory of the past, makes attachments to its judgments of its experiences and resists all attempts to move it out of its past... until it recognizes the captain of the ship of your life. Its attachments are both that which you fear most and that which you desire most... your aversions and your cravings. Your attachments resemble an unhealthy set of mooring lines or a spider's web that some of the people, places and things in your life have used to bind you down and take your power. Those unhealthy strands bind your ship of life to the wharf of your past. If you have managed to get under way, the unhealthy attachments have given the mainsheet and tiller to someone out of your past who owns you still. As long as someone else is at the helm they will try to get you to sail a course that is not your own. You are certain to run up on the rocks or find yourself in the eye of hurricane. You must be willing to take back your power and take over the wheel.

Please honor and respect your *responsibilities.* They lie in your established relationships to self and others to help meet needs of body, mind, soul, and spirit. You have taken them on, and they are not to be abandoned. Please acknowledge them. List them and describe them to your SoulCircle. In doing so, you are likely to recognize ways in which to make them as healthy as possible. All of them take time—your time—and you must validate your investment of time in meeting them. Do so, and you shall be the richer for it.

Your goals and intentions;

Your ego goes along with the particular crowd in which it feels secure. The ego is responsible for setting future goals, but does so infrequently.[88] A goal is a limit, a boundary, or a barrier; it is the line that you must cross with the football in order to score points. There is nothing beyond it. Having crossed it, you go back to neutral between the goal you defend and the one you strive for and begin the play all over again with the same goal in mind. This secular, tribal function gets little beyond accumulating points.

If someone else is navigating your ship, it must be her or his ego. If your ego wants control, then you are in an ego vs. ego combat and no lasting good can come from it. It will turn into a war and pointlessly destroy you both. This dilemma can only resolve itself when the ship's captain takes over the helm. Whereas your ego-*attachments* you hold you back, your soul-

responsibilities to other people, places and things that you accepted when you signed on for this journey can help you move forward.

Your soul and its intentions stand at the opposite pole from your ego. Passionate desire—the soul's *call*—opposes the ego's "gotta do it" *craving*. Your soul takes command with love, the power of spirit. Remember that souls come here to love, to *be* loved, or to *teach* love. Your love of the other will touch that person's soul and release it from you. Your willing release of the others frees you both from your past. This is forgiveness.

On the other hand, your soul came here with an intention that directs your attention, for the Latin root word, *intendere*, means to stretch toward... what a wonderful way to direct attention! Intention is a process like success that keeps extending (stretching) beyond that which you have achieved up to this point. In this regard, intention uses this powerful mantram: "Today, I am doing my best; tomorrow, I will do better!" Intention gives you an aiming point on the horizon of achievement. As you move toward it, it beckons to you. It calls your soul to a Universal adventure. The intentional journey is personal, soul-centered, and sacred—independent of the tribe, and yet contributing to it.

Your intention is what you want to have happen—what you want to see come of any situation—when the time is right. It is your true focus or call; an aim that guides action; an objective to which you direct attention. This is the nature of your service to humankind and, accordingly, to the whole Universe. It is a birthright of your soul. When you pay attention to your talents and passion in shaping an intention, you find your calling in life.

Your calling in life is your *work*. It is never a job. Your "job" is simply a way of putting bread on the table and clothes on your body without any necessary spiritual investment. Your talents can also have a direct bearing on your choice of a job but without any spiritual investment. Remember the Zen expression, "Before enlightenment, chop wood and carry water. After enlightenment, chop wood and carry water." Put your ego's "job" in a spiritual context, and it identifies with your soul's "work." This shift in the way you see yourself reveals many diamonds in those beautiful acres with which you were born.

Your will:

A central axis connects these two poles of intention and attachment—your will. The energy of creation that God gave us depends on your will for its success. The will comprises four qualities: strength, skill, ethics, and spirit.[89] As ego might direct it, it has strength and skill. Ego can corrupt the ethics of will to satisfy its perceived needs, denying the presence of spirit. As the soul, knowing the Good and the Truth and serving as the divine messenger, might direct it, it has power and grace. The soul provides the ethical and transpersonal, spiritual qualities of will.

Will is the mental property by which you choose a course of action. Such a choice is always deliberate. Will is essential to movement and creativity. Without will, you cannot get out of your attachments and move to your intention. Will is like the power in the engine of your automobile. Your engine might be capable of putting out 300 horsepower, but if your will is such that you don't even have your foot on the accelerator, your engine is at idle, turning out perhaps five horsepower. Or the 300 horsepower engine that normally runs on twelve cylinders has eleven disconnected sparkplug wires and can hardly idle. You have plugged the disconnected wires into the people, places, and things of your past that seem to have hurt you and kept you from moving. When you step on the accelerator, you have only one cylinder working and you are not going anywhere with it. Reclaim your energy from your past and focus it on what you want to have happen. Connect the wires to the spark plugs… you will become whole.

Soul and ego, a further contrast:

As the ego reaches out from its limited perspective to try to control its environment, its attachments to the past limit its abilities to exert control. As the soul extends from its Universal perspective, it empowers its environment and thereby removes all limits to personal creativity. The soul's transpersonal power extends over and beyond the ego's personal power with love, compassion, and forgiveness. The soul's presence transforms the ego's attachments into *responsibilities*. The energy flow along the axis of will is balanced. The archetypal power of the talents, temperament, and core passion flow without limit along the will axis, and the intention at its apex glows on the horizon, calling us to it.

As it is for you in this whole organization of ego and the soul, so is it for all of us. As it is for the microcosm, so it is for the macrocosm. As it is for the unique individual, so it is for the oneness of all human kind. The transformation of our world lies in the personal transformation of each of us... connected to our souls' creativity, and expressed in our service.

Ego creativity functions on a me-first, win-lose model of who sells the most product. Soul creativity functions on an equal partnership, win-win model of living in service. The ego model shuns service and servitude, equating them with slavery. The soul model respects and admires them, equating them with respect and honor, as in Jesus' humble act of washing his disciples' feet.

By forgiving—releasing yourself and others from the ties that bind, the plugs that disempower—you free yourself to use the strengths you developed from your woundedness to empower your will and direct your life toward worthy goals or ideals. You now take command of your ship of state. In this way, you become successful and are in a position to enjoy the material and emotional rewards of success.

There you have the elements of this process that introduce you to your acres of diamonds. You need now to call together your circle of friends who make up your SoulCircle, show and tell them your story, and describe your inventory. Ideally, they, too, have created their own story and inventory, and you can all share together in the dynamic of a SoulCircle.

Take your time. Savor your experience. You are worth every minute of it. When you are done, you may wish to move directly into the next phase of the process. It will take less than thirty minutes to complete

Clarifying Your Intent:

As I said above, the original meaning of intend is "to stretch toward." So, toward what would you like to stretch for the rest of your life? A boy born into a lawyer family expressed a love of the violin when he was still in his crib. His mother responded. His father rejected it because the life of a "fiddler" was a life of no money. The boy was forced to follow a law career, but continued to study the violin. In his mid-thirties, he found he had a malignant lymphoma and was given two years to live. He resigned from the law firm, told his father that he was going to spend the rest of his life playing his violin, and, five years later, he was concertmaster of the city's symphony... without any signs of lymphoma! What happened when he decided to stretch himself toward a career of playing the violin in a symphony orchestra?

I asked a wonderful woman with cancer who came to a H.O.P.E. Group with about three months to live what she planned to do with those three months. She said, "I don't know; I'm dying."

I responded with, "It seems that three months is a long time to spend dying. Perhaps there is something vitally important you would like to do for the next two months and three weeks and then spend only a week dying.

"Is that possible?" she asked.

"I don't know, but perhaps you do," I replied.

In response to her "How can I?" I suggested that she examine her life to see if there was something "vitally important" for her to do. She followed that suggestion, and when she came back the next week, she had her answer. She went back on chemotherapy, her cancer went into partial, yet satisfactory, remission, she got her work done in *four years* and died of a pneumonia that lasted less than a week!

I visited her in her home one month before she died. She looked wonderful. Her skin and hair glowed; and her eyes sparkled as she said, "The last four years have been the most wonderful years of my life, and I know they would not have been possible were it not for the first fifty. They seemed so hard at times, but looking back, if I had to do it all over again, I would not change a single thing! I couldn't have done the last four years without the first fifty!"

My friend was not cured of her cancer; she was healed— whole of body, mind, soul, and spirit. She had set an intention and she followed it with a passion. Setting, holding, and moving toward an intention bring meaning, value, and purpose to all life. Indeed, I sense a growing agreement that our universe exists because of a divine Intention to *be*. There is growing awareness that modeling our lives after the life of the Universe has its own built-in rewards. Virtually all great successful people for centuries have shared in knowing this fundamental fact of success[90].

Intention shares the dimensions of space and time with the rest of the physical Universe. It is also a process or method. Stating an intention is similar to saying a prayer. I know a woman who intended to get a new car and described it while she was driving up the turnpike only to come within an inch of serious injury in the accident that destroyed her old car. The accident was not her fault, so she had the car she had just finished describing within two days, thanks to the generosity of the other driver's insurance company. She had been specific about the space, her car, and nonspecific about the time and the method for getting rid of the old one!

When I was eleven, I set the intention to find out what love is; I have been working on that one ever since. When I was twenty-one, I set the intention of getting into medical school, setting in motion a process that would take eighteen months. Getting an interview with the Dean at McGill was the first step in the process. Getting into Rutgers was the second step. Getting straight A's through two semesters of four courses in pre-medical sciences each was the third. When I met the woman who is today my wife of forty years, the intention lit up like a light bulb in the first five

minutes of our first meeting. The two-year long courtship that led to our marriage was indeed a process. She and I set an intention of where we would like to live when we were in Iowa, finishing my surgical residency. We realized the intention *five years later,* and we have been living here ever since!

Think back over the processes of your life. Think of the times when you set intentions and how they materialized. It is time for another. This time, you will create a picture of your intention—that glimmer on the horizon—that beckoning muse. It will be a picture of that worthy goal or ideal that assures you of success. It develops out of your story held in the light of your form, talents, temperament, passion and will. *And you will draw a picture of it right now.* It can be as literal or symbolic as you want—any picture works.

Make your image symmetrical and symbolic—it is a *mandala* (a "geometric design symbolic of the universe.")[91] It is fun to try your hand at expressing your soul's intention this way. Give your heart and mind free rein with this, for you can only do it *right.* Let it be as symbolic as you wish so you can meditate on it, especially as you practice affirming this over time.

You only need to relax deeply into your recent small group experience and an intention will begin to form up your intention in your subconscious. Let your mind go into the nurturing space you have created for yourself and in which the members of your small group have held you. Let your mind bring up and examine that which you have created with the help of friends. Sit still in silence or play some soft music or go for a quiet walk, and it will take just a few minutes for this image to develop fully.

As soon as the image begins to come up in your mind, take the second sheet of easel paper and your drawing materials and let the image flow onto the paper. When you are done, set it aside and go immediately to the next part of this exercise.

Affirming Yourself:

This is the final step in SoulCircling—empowering your intention with an affirmation. Go into silence again in front of your mandala. Let a word come up, which describes the most direct action that you can take in order to realize your intention. This word or phrase is an affirmation, which means, literally, *to strengthen.* What we focus on expands, so you can imagine what twenty-one daily repetitions[92] of your affirmation will do to install that image in both your conscious and your subconscious mind!

A simple sentence (subject, verb, and object) repeated aloud to yourself where you can see your face and hear your words make the most powerful affirmations. You are the subject, so name yourself. You are seeing, hearing, or feeling what you want, so use the appropriate verb. State the object of your intention clearly, even if you believe (as we all are prone to do) that you are never going to make it. Do not worry; three weeks of repetition will change you. It is the magical time frame for getting any intention locked into the chemistry of your brain.

Ah, yes, you will change… and that is scary. However, it is the reason you got into SoulCircling in the first place… the old ways were no longer working well. The structure that your finite ego thought it could impose on life had begun to come apart at the seams. Your eternal soul with its depth of compassion can embrace and reassure your ego while it leads the way back to the constancy of change that inheres in the Universe. Trust it.

What I have to say next, I direct at your ego. Your soul knows all this already, and it knows, too, that to read about such things helps in understanding them.

Chapter 9: Moving on

"The most secure way is indeed the most insecure way. The way in which the richness of the quest accumulates is the right way. To find the right way is to follow your own bliss."

—Joseph Campbell

Principle:

- The soul and the egos with which it works provide God with a gift of life in return for God's gift of the life to that soul and those egos.

The Homecoming Way

Give your ego credit for trying to create a secure way for your whole life up to this point. The insecure way has worked well for your soul and for God since time began. Your soul knows the way in which the richness of the quest accumulates—it is in its earth orders—and your ego has now agreed to follow that way. Bliss, the ecstasy of salvation, is spiritual joy (American Heritage Dictionary). The path to bliss lies in inner peace, the peace that goes beyond understanding... the peace known to the soul that transforms the ego's ravening into a burning desire.

Change is the most consistent constant in the universe. In this chapter, I shall show you a pattern to life's changes that helps understand how we got to where we are and why the future will be so different. We shall come to understand how important it is that we take what we have learned about ourselves and use it to clarify an intention for our lives—today—for this is the only day to live.

A process-pattern of life

Did you ever wonder how you got from a fresh, single cell to a complex and beautifully organized multicellular adult human being? How in the name of Heaven did it do all this? Well, Heaven knows, and It gives us the means with which to discover this miracle. Those who explore these wonders view it as a *systematic process.* Gus Jaccaci, my gifted artist-friend, taught me to view this as a four-step process of *gathering, repeating, sharing, and transforming.*

Let me take you through it, using human embryology as a beautiful example. First, though, I must point out the existence of a barrier between the repeating and the sharing that the developing life must pass or die. Every individual and every species must pass this barrier if it is to survive.

When you were this tiny little cell, freshly formed by the union of your mother's egg and your father's sperm, you drifted passively inside one of your mother's two Fallopian tubes, propelled by gentle waves of specialized fingers that surrounded you with fluids rich in nutrients necessary for your life. You actively *gathered* the nutrients, and your inner, living processes made more of your inner stuff and you got bigger.

When you were so big you thought you were going to burst, a wonderful change occurred… you made two of everything, separated them off into two regions inside of you, and you ran a wall down between them. You *repeated* yourself! You were now two cells, but you stayed stuck together, and the two went on gathering more nutrients from your mother. Your two became four; your four became eight, your eight became sixteen, and they became thirty-two. Now they changed….

The thirty-two created a space in their middle. They also started to become different—they started to behave as if they had a front, a back, two sides, a top, and a bottom. The cells were different from each other, and they had to cooperate—*share*—their new identities with each other. Now you were also so big the Fallopian tube had to get rid of you. You had been sending your mother chemical messengers about your progress, and she was making room for you in her womb. "Pop!" out of the tube and into a space that might not like you, you genetically strange new thing (your DNA is different from your mother's). You had to share yourself with your mother or pass on out through the cervix and die. You did it, my friend, you crossed that barrier between repeating and sharing... only half of all conceptions make it past this barrier!

Your mother's womb was even better suited to nurture your continued growth than was that Fallopian tube where you lived for a few days before taking this great leap into the unknown. You now grew at a tremendous rate by gathering and repeating in the sharing space of that womb. In no time at all, you had a completely new shape—you had *transformed* into an *embryo*, with cells busily making all of your organs from your skin to your brain and from your eyes to your gut.

You would continue with this systematic process for about another eight weeks until all of your organs were hooked up and working—sharing responsibilities for all of those bodily functions that you would need for the rest of your life. If one of the organ systems was not working, you would have died—your mother would have *miscarried* you... and one out of ten human pregnancies ends this way.

However, you plucky, wonderful little *fetus*, you got it all right and you went back to gathering and repeating in the new sharing relationships for the next test of your sharing ability: your birth and the necessity of being able to share yourself with a totally new and different environment, the air. Once again, my friend, you crossed that barrier successfully, though some others did not. Welcome to the world, little *infant!*

The gather, repeat, share, and transform did not stop here. As an infant you had to gather and repeat the input of its senses to learn how to take the measure of the physical world with its sights, sounds, smells, tastes, and skin feelings. That took about six months. You also had to measure the emotional tone of the people in your environment. In this way, you shared yourself with your human environment and you transformed into a *child* over the next four to five years.

You spent the next seven or eight years gathering and repeating knowledge and experience in order to develop your mind, your body, and your ego. Suddenly, as you approached your teen years, your hormones hit, forcing you into a new set of relationships—another sharing. This transformed you into an adolescent, and if you lived in a tribe with a strong wisdom tradition, you would have had a rite of passage into the life of collaboration of soul and ego—a new sharing that would transform you into an adult ready for your spiritual development. In all likelihood, that did not happen. Your ego was left alone to navigate in a world of disconnected humans also following an ego path, and you've been coping with your need to be in relationship with others ever since. You have been looking for the sharing space all along, somehow knowing that our spirituality depends on our relationships with each other. Your search is identical to three hundred years of searching for the soul of our species.

All along this path of yours how many ceremonies welcomed you into the new world of each transformation? If there were as many as mine, there were only a few, and they were a bit distorted. Mine consisted of getting my driver's license, graduating from high school, becoming old enough to get drunk, and, finally, graduating from college. Would it not be appropriate to have had ceremony with elders and peers at each of these occasions to welcome the new you who has just crossed the barrier? Perhaps you would like to design a ceremony with your SoulCircle to celebrate your recent transformation, for you know that it is never too late to take the spiritual path. You have just demonstrated that to your Self and to other Selves. As a one-of-a-kind work of art, you *are* worthy of that ceremony. Enjoy it.

Now, as you move forward into the rest of your life, keep in mind that you have just had a good look at the effects of human beings sharing themselves with each other. How does it feel? Do you like it? Would you like others to feel as you do? If so, share what you have learned with us in H.O.P.E. Let us work with you in the sharing space. Work with others to develop their move across the big barrier. Be a virus of health and healing. Help the epidemic grow.

Let us now look at what we have achieved in a new light and rewrite the Garden of Eden allegory....

Epilogue: Eden, the City of Soul

Out beyond ideas of wrongdoing and rightdoing, there is a field. I'll meet you there.

— *Jalaluddin Rumi*

God utters me like a word containing a partial thought of himself.

—*Thomas Merton,*
New Seeds of Contemplation

Time means nothing. Time is just the way we measure the gaps between not knowing something and knowing it, or not doing something and doing it.

—*Richard Bach*

Eternity is not an everlasting flux of time, but time is a short parenthesis in a long period.

—*John Donne*

Our duty as humans is to behave as if limits to our abilities do not exist, for we are collaborators in creation.

—*Teilhard de Chardin*

Considerations:

Consider what you have just done for yourself:
- You have explored your secular and spiritual sides.
- You have had the opportunity to take a deep, soul-searching look at your life, its story, and its resources.
- You have had the opportunity to work with other human beings in a supportive, synergistic environment.
- You have gained insights into yourself and others.

Epilogue

- You have a good sense of the meaning and value of intention and you have created one for yourself.
- You know the practical use of affirmation.

Consider how this might apply to our wonderful species. What is our story… told and listened to with love and compassion? What do our species' acres of diamonds look like? What resources of talent and temperament do we share? What are our human passions? What is our will?

As I look at our acres of diamonds, I come to but one conclusion; the Godhead wants us to go to the stars. Today, in terms of our human story, is a time of great upheaval and change. Many write about it, aware that something is in the wind. James Burke, in his book, *The Day the Universe Changed*,[93] does a wonderful job of pointing out to us that such times of upheaval have occurred in our past with remarkable regularity—multiple transformations. He brings us into the scientific present through ten of these major changes, and points out at the end that Buddhism and Science both seek "the single force that unites the universe." While science on the one hand seeks that source in the external (*outer*) universe, Buddhism seeks it in the *inner* realms beyond mind and thought. I infer from him that tomorrow needs to bring the outer and the inner together. This, to me, is and always has been the work of the soul; so let us explore the deep measure of the soul.

How deep are the dimensions of the soul? How many stories about the soul are there today? How many were experienced but never talked about in past years? Such a depth boggles our imaginations. It is time we let The Great Mystery boggle our imaginations. We Westerners used to allow ourselves to be boggled, but our fascination with science as the way to all understanding puts limits on our thinking; for science defines things. The discomfort of boggling is outdated, and our newfound awe and amazement have replaced its fearfulness; for The Mystery never left us… we only left It.

We are certainly the most diverse, creative species this Earth has ever created. Driven by our insatiable curiosity and need to understand, we have developed these multifaceted, powerful qualities into a great strength, the power of creation. However, we have put ourselves at risk of self-annihilation because of this power. We are both blessed and cursed by it. To survive, we must turn every iota of this power into a blessing.

We shall succeed as soon as we remember that our strengths and talents are a Gift of the Divine. We shall then come to know that we can live consecrated lives.

Through finding out our spiritual nature, we can align our lives to the Life that is The Source of all Being. We do not have to believe in a "God", a "Big Bang", a "Ground of Being", or a "Great Spirit" in order to find in ourselves the awareness that we are part of a living Universe that gave us our lives. We must know, moreover, that the Universe is more than just a Body of planets, gas, and space: it is also a Mind that connects with thoughts, a Soul with a passion, and a Spirit that breathes its Being into all.

As we align to the Spirit, we will become more comfortable with things that seem to be unresolved opposites: the simple and the complex; the spirit and the soul; the masculine and the feminine; the imminent and the manifest. We will come to realize that when we hold each polar opposite together in dynamic relationship, they create a field of creative tension in which we can chose to dance, and in so doing, we can let ourselves be drawn beyond these opposites to fields of even greater awareness.

We have been there already, for we have names for That Which Lies Beyond: Ground of Being, Void, Tao, Source, Godhead, etc. The names are weak, inadequate labels for That Which Has No Name, No Face, No Form, and No Mind. It is pure awareness and potential. It knows itself—all of its form and mind. It is Magnificence. It is Love. It is Holiness. There is nothing It is not. It simply Is.

How do we find It? We go beyond the limits of where we are now and where we have been for countless thousands of years. We go beyond body and mind to soul. We go beyond body, mind, and soul to spirit. We go beyond these four to find It. We have been told how to find It. "Be still," is the commandment. So, let us learn to be still. So, let us learn to forget all that we thought we knew about It and ourselves. The instant we do, It will show us of Itself... and we will know It. When we come to know It, our relationship with It will have changed beyond our ability to imagine.

My friend Larry Fournier was aware of his spiritual connection when he was seven. He was one of those children who never forget where they come from. He knew that he would serve God for the rest of his life. His ego was already strong, leading him through endless challenges. Priests and family treated him as if he could not fail, nurturing his ego by giving him intellectual challenges far beyond what was asked of his classmates. He was hard to get along with at times because of his unflagging determination to do challenging things, and yet he is a much-loved man to this day. He is loved because his ego and his soul work in harmony with each other. They have worked together in a wonderful relationship for most of his life. Larry has come home to himself. It has been a long process... and a rewarding one.

There is but one word that describes homecoming—love. Love is not an abstract concept. Its emotional name is joy, which manifests in the form of specific messenger molecules that flood the nerve connections throughout our brains and spinal cords as we experience it. Special nerves connect our brains to the wall of the small intestine that manufactures this chemical and pours it into the bloodstream. This red flow carries it in turn to every cell in the body, where it literally turns on the immune function inherent in every cell. We need love to live. Experience love, feel joy, and every cell of your body knows it.

Love's wondrous, universal power leads me to offer you the following:

> The ancient wisdom of our wonderful species tells us that when we choose to develop our lives on a web of love, we will know joy that few can imagine.

Our Own Homecoming:

The time has come in our evolution that we come home to who we really are—what Creation designed us for—and recognize our acres of diamonds. All the materials are in place. We know our bodies are holographic fragments of the body of the Creation, our minds are holographic fragments of the mind of the Creation, our spirit is a holographic fragment of the spirit of Creation, and the soul we put aside a few centuries ago is a holographic fragment of the soul of the Creation.

We made the choice to set our spiritual connection aside in order to find out how creative—and destructive—our ego could be without any spiritual guidance. Without any awareness of the divine Whole of which we are a vital part, we became competitors in creation. We had to, for the emotion of the ego is fear, the underlying motive for competition. The response to fear is anger, for we came to believe that the best defense is a good offense. Consequently, we took the life-giving energy of the sun and made the life-destroying hydrogen bomb. The time has come to stop competing with the Creator and join It in Its passion for being. It is time to reopen the dialog with our souls.

The emotion of the soul is love. All seven billion of us must harness the emotional energy of our souls and commit to collaborating with the Creator, the Godhead, in the act of Creating. Some cabalists, Jewish mystics, are wont to use the expression "God-ing"[94] to describe the ongoing, creative process we call the universe. God-ing demands participation of us, for it is an active term. The Godhead wants us to use our gifts of body, mind, soul, and spirit to join It in the very act of Creation, itself. That is God-ing.

Our agile minds have had a hunger for knowledge ever since our Source gave us Its fruit. The responsive flow of knowledge was at first a trickle, just fast enough then for us to handle it. The trickle increased to a rivulet, and a passion to understand the wonder of the physical universe arose in our hearts hundreds of years ago. The rivulet became a stream. Since then, the flow of information into our minds has widened into a huge river—and we are still able to handle it. At times when it has threatened to overwhelm us, we have developed concerns about the whelming, the watery flow, and the flood slowed down in response to our concerns. The intentional, participatory Universe knows us because It created us, and It responds to the desires It built into us. Arrogant naiveté leads us to believe we stole knowledge from The Source, and it is arrogant to believe that we are in control of its flow today. Our place in the world is an important part of this flow.

We are to use this knowledge for the good of the Universe by starting at home with ourselves and all other life forms as caught up in the flow of life as we are. Insights into who we are, as persons, will clarify our roles in helping our species realize its potential, as we are bound to that of the Creation itself. This evolution follows a natural cycle of growth—gathering, repeating, sharing, and transforming—a healing cosmology of four concentric circles, personal, tribal, social, and universal.

We are coming to a greater understanding of the Godhead that is God, male; Goddess, female; and God, ground of being, neither masculine nor feminine, and yet both. Thus, it speaks to the poles of a paradox and the more fundamental intention that lies behind and gives rise to both of them. "God" and "Goddess" are the poles of the most significant paradox we have ever known. What intention gives rise to them? Eventually, as we pursue every paradox to its resolution, we shall encounter a process that has no opposite. All paradoxes come to resolution within It.

Einstein said that every point in the Universe is at the exact center of its universe. Ego fundamentally disagrees with this statement because ego thinking proclaims but one center of the universe—itself. I pointed out earlier that ego is exclusionary and separatist. Therefore, if my ego is the center of the Universe, yours cannot be quite so central.

The soul, on the other hand, accepts Einstein's statement as truth. It sees each soul it encounters as the exact center of its universe. Its ability to love without condition makes possible the recognition of soul-centered universes, all of which have equal value in the Universe that is the Creation, Itself.

Ultimately, our divine potential leads us to become collaborators in creation, authors of volumes of universal experience comprising encyclopedias that lead us to our Source. When the last volume in each encyclopedia recognizes its identity with The Source, the cowl folds back from Its beautiful face and the soul sees itself mirrored in Its eyes. The soul writes "finis" on the last page of the volume and closes the book, which then pours the creative energy of its entire experience into Being… we now go to the stars and a new gathering begins.

Genesis 3, reprise:

The Godhead in Its passionate intention for *Being* became Mother-Goddess and Father-God, and the Universe was born. It needed to know Itself, so it made woman and man. It made them different but equal. It saw that this was good and It placed them in a lovely garden with all they would need.

In the center of the garden, It placed a tree whose fruit contained all knowledge of good and evil. It sent Its divine servant, Serpent, to invite Its children to partake of this fruit, knowing the immediate consequences. Having eaten of the fruit the woman and the man began to play with the resources of the garden. They made mistakes and their childish use of knowledge made them believe that they were bad. Thus their ego was born.

In the self-punishment of their egos, the woman and the man banished themselves from the garden, so the Godhead placed a spinning, shining beacon over the entrance and a cherub at either side to wait for their return. The beacon would give all of Its children's children a light they could see from over the horizon. It promised them the way home, and the cherubim would welcome them when they came back.

The Godhead sent beings—angels—to subtly, gently guide Its children through danger past death, back to the garden of life and love with the knowledge of why It had created them. After

Epilogue

many, many years, the Creator's children felt the compassionate, forgiving presence of Its angel messengers who brought Its love. They raised their heads from their labors, the woman in childbearing and the man in the fields, and they saw the light on the horizon calling them.

They picked up their beds and followed the light. They saw the shining beacon and the smiling faces of the welcoming committee. They walked through the great, open gate and saw in the beauty of the garden what they had not seen before—a Universal City—a stairway to the stars rising from every rooftop.

They had come home… they knew their journey had just begun.

RECOMMENDED SOUL READING

Barasch, Marc Ian, *The Healing Path: A Soul Approach to Illness.* New York: J P Tarcher, 1994

Moore, Thomas, *Care of the Soul: A Guide for Cultivating Depth and Sacredness in Everyday Life.* New York: HarperCollins, 1994

Mountain Dreamer, Oriah, *The Invitation.* San Francisco: Harper, 1999

Myss, Carolyn, *Sacred Contracts.* New York: Random House Harmony, 2002

Small, Jacquelyn, *Rising to the Call.* Marina del Rey, CA: De Vorss, 1997

Tolle, Eckhardt, *The Power of Now.* Novato, CA: New World, 1999

Zukav, Gary, *The Seat of the Soul.* New York: Simon and Schuster, 1989

Index

Notes

[1] Jacqelyn Small, LMSW, founder of Eupsychia Institute for Well-Being (www.eupsychiainc.com), offers trainings in soul-based psychology.

[2] For practical purposes, we put the wiring for this program in a thickening at the upper end of the spinal cord where all incoming sensory and outgoing motor nerves gather because it would only take up precious time to go to the thinking-feeling areas in the outer cortex of the brain in order to find the response to the threat.

[3] Lonice Bias, respected teacher of our young in recognizing and correcting the application of knowledge, introduced me to this concept in a talk she gave to the middle and high school students of our district. She had experienced the tragedy of losing two lovely sons, one due to self-inflicted drug use, and the other to the bullets of a stalker. She saw that each had lost his life because of the misapplication of knowledge. The first had misapplied his own knowledge and the second had died because of another person's misapplication of knowledge.

[4] One of the nine daughters of Mnemosyne and Zeus, created to celebrate the victory of the Olympians over the Titans. They were the patron goddesses of poets, musicians, the liberal arts, and sciences.

[5] You could develop these insights with a personal coach, who would likely show you that you are no longer simply trying to "manage stress;" you are discovering how to manage your life. The personal and professional coaching field is growing, providing people with increased self-awareness and stress management skills that are better called "life management skills." Most of these coaches are trained in giving productive and cost-effective telephone consultations. A web site search using the key words "personal coach," professional coach," and "life coach" produces hundreds of web pages.

6 6245 West Howard St. Niles, IL 60714. 1-800-525-9000

[7] "As ye sow, so shall ye reap." "What goes 'round comes 'round."

[8] New York: Harper & Row, 1986.

[9] *On Death and Dying.* New York: MacMillan, 1969.

[10] As I talk about intention in this book, it is not surprising to know that the wealthy couple who owned the house had intended its health use in the 1940's. He died in 1945, and the intention was clearly stated in his will. It was also present in her will at the time of her death in 1965. The trust took care of her nurse/companion until her death in 1987, at which time the trust had also been making considerable gifts to the hospital of which I had been

a staff member. All of their gifts continue to this day, wonderfully realizing their intention to serve the health of the community.

[11] Your temperament comprises those mental and physical characteristics that help distinguish you. Your temperament is the way you choose to navigate life. Simply put, the four humors of old medicine are four ways of expressing temperament: sanguine (happy, energetic), choleric (angry), phlegmatic (calm, unemotional), and melancholic (sad).

[12] Astrophysicists are scientists who work with the BIG numbers of the universe (like the total number of atoms in it), and they estimate that in the space of time between 10^{-35} and 10^{-33} seconds after the first spark lit up, the universe expanded 10^{43} times over-almost instantaneously, and certainly faster than the speed of light! If you boggle at that number, remember that the little number called the exponent represents the number of zeroes after the number, "1," if you were to write it out. Therefore, 1×10^3 is the same as 1,000. Forty-three zeroes would reach halfway across this page! A negative exponent such as used to describe these tiny fractions of time means that the big number is divided into the number "1," so 10^{-3} is the same as 1/1000 and 10^{-35} would be written out as "1" over another "1" followed by thirty-five zeroes, which would reach almost as far!

[13] There is enough hydrogen in our star, the one we call Sun, to keep this fire burning for another ten billion years… plenty of time for us to do the work we are put here to do!

[14] It is estimated that our galaxy comprises close to 100 billion stars. Our galaxy is one of as many as 60 billion galaxies making up one galactic cluster of which there may be as many as 60 billion more clusters! These are big numbers that make the probability of us being the only God-loving living entities in the universe pretty darn small.

[15] The invention of the incandescent light bulb by Thomas Edison typifies the result of exercising this power of focus. Out of knowledge that electricity could make metal wires glow a dull red, he dreamed of a durable, brightly glowing filament hundreds of times brighter than a candle flame. The clarity of this image supported him through ten thousand tries before he got one filament to glow brightly without burning up.

[16] The Great Invocation is a gift to us from the mystic, Alice Bailey.

[17] Albert Einstein and two of his colleagues at Princeton University, Boris Podolsky, and Nathan Rosen asked essential theoretical questions in 1935 that led to several exquisite quantum physical experiments that showed that information was transmitted between sub-atomic particles at immeasurable, supraluminal speeds.

[18] There is evidence that indicates the existence of some genetic variations between identical twins. They certainly show different responses to their environment. The recent completion of the human genome project

may well provide us with much clearer answers to these questions. Identical twins are clones. The chances of accidental cloning is one in several billion, and if you were to meet your clone on the street, you would undoubtedly recognize her or him, but if you two were to share a cup of coffee, you would find out how different you are. You have lived in different environments with different passions, and so it is with identical twins, whose environmental differences may be minute in their developing years, but enlarge as they mature and follow their passions.

Chapter Two

[19] Britannica CD 98 Multimedia Edition © 1994-1998 by Encyclopædia Britannica, Inc.

20 "Talent" includes the many forms of intelligence that Howard Gardner has so well described in his book, *Intelligence Reframed: Multiple Intelligences for the 21st Century.* New York: Basic, 1993.

First, the intelligences that we are used to finding on standard IQ tests; intelligences that appear to relate to purely mental processes:

- o   Intelligence of logic and mathematics enables a person to detect patterns, think logically, and exercise reason.
- o   Intelligence of language is the ability to express oneself with the written and/or spoken word.

Second, three intelligences that appear to relate to perceptions of external patterns:

- o   Spatial intelligence describes our ability to see patterns in space, whether it is wide-open or closed, so a pilot and a chess player both have spatial intelligence.
- o   Bodily-Kinesthetic intelligence relates to the ability to use the body and its movements creatively, either in part or in whole. Dancers and athletes typify this form of intelligence.
- o   Musical intelligence relates to the ability to recognize musical pitch and rhythm and to perform and/or compose music.

Third, two intelligences of person:

- o   Interpersonal intelligence that reflects a person's to respond to the feelings, motivations, and intentions of others—the external world.
- o   Intrapersonal intelligence reflects a person's ability to work apprehensively and creatively from and with the internal world.

Daniel Goleman has added emotional intelligence in his book, *Emotional Intelligence,* New York: Bantam, 1997.

[21] Our temperament comprises those thoughts and behaviors with which we usually interact with others: happiness, sorrow, anger, depression, directness, indirectness, cheerfulness, etc.

[22] Ego, as a concept, goes back thousands of years, but Freud gave it the psychological emphasis that appeals to Western minds about 100 years ago.

[23] Before the human genome project finished with its listing of our genes, we believed there were about 100,000 of the little clusters of energy that determined our physical qualities. At the end of the project, that number dropped to 30,000! We knew there was lots of silent space in the chromosomes, but now there seems to be much more. Could it be that the silent space is somehow vitally important, and that it prevents us from cloning ourselves by introducing room for all sorts of variables in evolution?

[24] This little "guilt trip" is meant to underscore the importance of not making mistakes like wandering out into water over my head. It works in the realm of ego, using the past in an attempt to create a better future, but it does so by saying. "You made a mistake, and you should have known better." As we use it, it punishes—by shaming.

[25] Societies that practice shunning use it as a capital punishment... the punished one simply fades away because of the unbearable pain of total rejection, and death usually comes within six months.

[26] As I learned more about traditional and contemporary spiritual practices, they repeatedly asked me to examine my perceptions, or how my senses see, hear, taste, smell, and feel things. Medical science knows that our senses are limited. Our eyes cannot see the ultraviolet that bees and birds see. Our ears cannot hear the low frequency sounds by which elephants communicate. We cannot hear the high-pitched tones easily heard by dogs and cats. We do not respond to pheromones in the same way that animals and insects do. We cannot take the full measure of anything with these quantitatively limited senses that are built into our nervous systems.

[27] I learned this acronym from the Twelve Step program of Alcoholics Anonymous as I experienced it in several years of participating in an ACOA (adult children of alcoholics) Al-Anon group.

[28] If you want help in learning this, I recommend that you get Daniel Goleman's book, *Emotional Intelligence* (New York: Bantam, 1995). It is an excellent resource for choosing the emotions with which we would like to respond to any given situation.

Chapter Three

[29] Many people have reflected on the conflict between Jew and Arab that seems to have begun in Abraham's tent 4,200 years ago when Sarah exiled Hagar and her son, Ishmael, who became the father of the Arab tribes which gave birth to Mohammad.

[30] Henry J. M. Nouwen, the mystical Dutch priest, gave me this beautiful image of "who" I am in an audio tape called *Who are We?* published and for sale by Ave Maria Press, P.O. Box 428, Notre Dame, IN 46556, www.avemariapress.com.

[31] The Merriam-Webster's Collegiate Dictionary, 10th edition (© 1994) and the American Heritage Dictionary, 3rd edition (© 1992) both define soul in the same way as the Encyclopedia Britannica.

[32] "I think, therefore I am." -Rene Descartes

[33] The solar plexus, the Sun Center, is one of the energy centers of the body called a chakra. It is the center of control, and, rightfully, the home of ego. Indeed, when your control is threatened, do you not feel it in your belly just above the navel?

[34] *Anam Cara.* New York: Harper, 1997

[35] Mill Valley, CA: Foundation for Inner Peace, 1992.

[36] The actress, singer, and author, Portia Nelson, wrote an exquisite piece about that hole called, An Autobiography in Five Short Chapters. Subsequently, she wrote a delightful little book called *There's a Hole in my Sidewalk* (Hillsboro, OR: Beyond Words, 1994) that includes the Autobiography, and gently, compassionately examines our repeated sufferings and the strange, often circular, ways of thinking that take us back into it.

[37] Psychiatry has been especially hard-hit by these constraints, and today's visit to a psychiatrist is less likely to be the one-hour talk session than an eight-minute encounter at ends up with the doctor handing over a piece of white paper with a prescription on it.

[38] Richard B. Weinberg, MD, a gastroenterologist at Bowman Gray Medical School asked this question of himself and a challenging patient. He describes the miraculous consequences beautifully in his article, *Communion.* (Annals of Internal Medicine 1995; 123:804-5)

[39] This may be a way of following William Osler's advice that we must "care more for the individual patient than for the special treatment of the disease.

[40] H.O.P.E. Groups' exemplar for this work is Victor Frankl's "(discovery) of the meaning of life in Auschwitz."

[41] Conventions of thought around the world make the mind masculine and the body feminine.

[42] American Heritage Dictionary defines religion and as "a. Belief in and reverence for a supernatural power or powers regarded as creator and governor of the universe. b. A personal or institutionalized system grounded in such belief and worship." Science certainly focuses its profound capabilities of investigation not on the "supernatural power" not on the creating and governing powers of the universe. Religions (like Buddhism) do not have to focus on "God" in order to be called a religion. In

fact, the Supreme Court of the United States classifies Buddhism as a "non-theist religion". Science belongs in the same category.

[43] Lewis Thomas, MD, the poet laureate of medicine in the last century, writes about medicine as a science in *The Youngest Science*. New York: Viking Press, 1983.

[44] Antoine de Saint-Exupéry. (1900 - 1944), was a French aviator and writer who was shot down on a reconnaissance mission over the Mediterranean. His works are poetic examinations of the life of adventure and danger unique to pilots and warriors. *The Little Prince*. New York: Harcourt, 2000, from which this quote is taken, is a child's fable for adults, with a gentle and grave reminder that the best things in life are still the simplest ones and that real wealth is giving to others. (from the Encyclopaedia Britannica, Copyright (c) 1995)

[45] Lonice Bias, respected teacher of our young in recognizing and correcting the application of knowledge, lost two lovely sons, one due to self-inflicted drug use, and the other to the bullets of a stalker. She saw that each had lost his life because of the misapplication of knowledge. The first had misapplied his own knowledge and the second had died because of another person's misapplication of knowledge.

[46] Friedrich Nietzsche had this to say about life's meaning: "it is more important to find out why you live than how you live." Viktor Frankl's experience in Nazi concentration camps fully substantiated Nietzsche's statement.

[47] A hologram is formed by placing a photographic film so that it squarely faces the object to be photographed. It is then exposed to a laser beam that has been split into two beams. The first passes through a diverging lens so that it illuminates the entire object, the reflected light from which falls on the film without an intervening , focusing lens. The second, called the reference beam, is sent through a similar lens over an identical distance, but in this case, it is reflected off a mirror so that it falls at an angle on the film. Because of the coherence of laser light, the two beams form interference patterns on the film, and no sensible image of the object is present on looking through it. However, if the developed film is illuminated by the reference beam at the same angle at which it originally struck the film, and an observer looks through the film thus illuminated, a virtual image of the object appears in exactly the place where the object had been originally!

[48] Keep in mind that all of us, women and men alike, have both masculine and feminine attributes.

[49] In her book by the same name (New York: Simon & Schuster, 1999), Pert describes these remarkable chemicals that turn feelings into bodily reactions.

[50] Fear is the engine of the survival response. The adrenal glands produce two of the most important of fear's chemicals, adrenaline, and cortisol. These chemicals are so important to us that we cannot live but minutes without them.

[51] The feelings of love are not associated with adrenal function but the gut and the heart that express it with their own highly specialized chemicals, such as the interferons, interleukins, and vasoactive intestinal peptide that collectively empower the immune system and resist invasion by potentially lethal organisms. Studies in orphanages at the turn of the twentieth century showed that love is essential for life. Orphaned infants whose only human contact came from adults who simply fed and clothed them died within six months; whereas those infants thrived when their caregivers held them in their arms and talked to them while feeding, bathing, and dressing them. Societies that practice shunning use it as a capital punishment, for victims of shunning seldom live past six months, unless they can find others who have been subjected to the same, marginalizing practice. In this case, they bond into their own community, finding love for each other—in their fear and hatred of the community that shunned them—with dire consequences for all.

[52] (1) right understanding—faith in the Buddhist view of the nature of being in terms of the Four Noble Truths that say, essentially, that to be human is to suffer, we suffer because we crave, we can get rid of the cravings, and this eight-fold way is the way to be rid of them; (2) right intention or thought—the resolve to practice the faith; (3) right speech—being open, honest, kind and truthful; (4) right action—abstaining from theft, from improper sexual behavior and from taking life; (5) right livelihood—choosing occupations in keeping with Buddhist principles; (6) right effort—choosing good mental states over bad ones; (7) right mindfulness—awareness of body, mind and emotions; and (8) right concentration—meditation. Of these eight, steps 1 and 2 comprise right wisdom (prajña); steps 3, 4, and 5 are right morality (shila); and steps 6, 7, and 8 are right concentration (samadhi).

[53] *No Man is an Island.* New York: Harcourt, Brace, Jovanovich, 1955

[54] There's that "mask" word again; implying that the personality is a cover-up of an essential reality.

[55] The word, individual, comes from the Latin with the meaning: "that which cannot be divided" and control works by dividing (divide and conquer) while power works by integrating.

[56] This is the first line of Alice Bailey's "Great Invocation," a copy of which can be obtained from the Lucis Trust, 120 Wall Street, 24th floor, New York, NY 10005.

[57] Adler, Mortimer. *How to Think about God.* New York: Bantam, 1980.

Chapter Four

[58] Our ego-rich, soul-poor society does not like to age. As I pointed out earlier, ego begins to tire and retire when it is about 35 years old, so any life beyond that is a weaker, less potent life, in the eye of ego. However, in soul-rich societies aging is a ripening and maturing process that leads to a quality product. Without this process, there could be no grapes, no wine, and no cheese, so let us keep in mind the benefits of aging: ripening and maturing.

[59] Older societies, not exposed to reason, still believe in soul. As we are all together in our humanity, it seems appropriate to respect their belief and even ask them to help us return to our own awareness of soul. As I look at the e-mail postings that cross my desk that refer to Native traditions of many kinds, I have no doubt that we have asked and have been heard.

[60] *Life after Life.* Atlanta: Mockingbird Books, 1975

[61] *The Omega Project.* New York: William Morrow, 1992, and *Heading Toward Omega.* New York: William Morrow, 1984.

[62] *Saved by the Light.* Rockland, MA: Harper Collins, 1994, is a remarkable autobiography of a man who was holding a telephone to his ear when lightning struck the telephone line. He was clinically dead for twenty-five minutes, and was in an intensely brilliant white light for that time. The story is about how the experience transformed his entire life.

[63] *Embraced by the Light.* Placerville, CA: Gold Leaf Press, 1992.

[64] Doctor Weiss made his experience public in his moving book, *Many Lives, Many Masters*, (New York: Simon and Schuster, 1988). At a Past life Regression training workshop in which I participated, he told us that his patient who was the protagonist of the book made him acutely aware of the validity of the concept of reincarnation. He was aware that reincarnation was not a part of his Jewish upbringing; so he looked back in Judaic history and found that there was just such a belief system until about 300 years ago. He looked into the belief systems of the other two "religions of the book," and found evidence of belief in reincarnation in both Christianity and Islam that also ended 300 years ago, roughly coinciding with the beginning of the age of reason!

[65] Michael wrote the classic, *The Way of the Shaman.*(San Francisco: Harper, 1990) to help western minds grasp this world-wide phenomenon.

[66] Michael Harner and Sandra Ingerman (q.v.) use this term in their trainings of Shamanic practices to describe the psychic state into which the Shaman enters in order to find help for the individual for whom s-he is trav-

traveling. Ordinary reality is primarily oriented to the function of our eyes. For most of us, the expression, "Seeing is believing," is the truth of all experience. How often do we hear someone who has witnessed something remarkable say, "If I hadn't seen it with my own eyes, I wouldn't have believed it!" Non-ordinary reality is a total sensory experience that brings the images from within, not from without. The seeing is not with the eyes. The hearing is not with the ears. The images come from another source than the world we usually experience with those senses.

[67] Some societies use psychedelics to help the shaman enter the desired altered state of consciousness. Our society's recreational use of such drugs makes it ill advised for us to attempt to use them for shamanic purposes. Someday we shall have the maturity to be able to use drugs for spiritual ritual beyond a sip of wine at communion, but for now, the drum, the didgeridoo, the musical bow must remain our instruments of choice for entering states of shamanic consciousness.

[68] Sandra is Director of Education for the Foundation for Shamanic Studies, PO Box 1939, Mill Valley, CA 94942-1939. Michael Harner, Ph.D., created the foundation based on his studies of the worldwide practice of Shamanism when he was an undergraduate psychology student. His early findings are described in his entertaining and informative book, *The Way of the Shaman* (San Francisco: Harper San Francisco, 1990)

[69] I do not wish to discuss whether there is such a presence of being in inanimate things, even though it does make an interesting argument.

[70] Deep process intensives help the participants heal by creating safe, caring environments for them to get in touch with and express the feelings of old traumas that had been blocked by the protective force of denial. Unblocking these feelings quite literally releases their pent up energy that is the cause of many mental and physical illnesses. Of necessity, the participant must go back through the traumatic experience and expose ego and soul to the old injury in hopes that the safe environment will free the blocked energy. This kind of work has undergone a lot of beneficial development over the years, and it has helped a good many people. There were some abusive intensives of this kind, but they were pretty well eliminated by the end of the 21st century.

[71] He describes his experiences in Man's Search for Meaning. Boston: Beacon Press, 1992.

[72] New York: Washington Square, 1999.

[73] From his autobiography, *Recollections*. (Cambridge, MA: Perseus, 2000)

[74] Incredible because of his age... polio was extremely rare in children less than three years old!

[75] In some indigenous spiritual traditions, the four cardinal directions are the four components of each human being. The east represents the spirit, south represents the emotions (soul), west represents the body, and north represents the mind.

[76] New York: Lothrop, Lee & Shepherd Co

[77] This expression, "SoulCircle" is not unique to soul work. I have seen others use it (usually as two words: "Soul Circle") since Gus Jaccaci and I put together the first Circling the Soul exercise and registered that name. It seemed natural to convert the more cumbersome name to "SoulCircling" as it pertains to the work I describe in this chapter. I wanted to register the name, but it was too close to other names that use the two words in many parts of the country. This implies that there is a growing consciousness of this soul work, and that all of us who use the term have much the same outcome in mind—helping people discover their own soul.

Chapter Seven

[78] The interaction of two or more agents or forces so that their combined effect is greater than the sum of their individual effects (American Heritage Dictionary).

[79] A member of the Religious Society of Friends. S-he would also likely be a member of a specific "monthly meeting," a body that usually meets weekly for worship and monthly to conduct its business. Friends' business includes matters of membership, finance, property, and deliberation on concerns raised by individual members or referred to it by superior meetings. Friends Meetings also have specific legal functions, such as the ability to marry people and issue marriage licenses. In the case that a couple wish to marry, they convene a clearness committee to help them clarify their intention to marry and hold that marriage "under the care of the Meeting."

[80] The word, concern, which comes from a Latin word meaning to mingle together, implies a personal involvement in the source of the causes of an anxiety—one's own or that of another.

[81] Religions are beliefs in supernatural powers. The Source of all things is certainly most wonderful, beautiful, and natural. It *is* Its Creation and not above it,—separate from it—which would make it "other than" Nature. God is in Nature, Nature is in God, and we are in error when we try to make the source and being of nature *super*natural. We will get a much greater appreciation of God when we consider It to be perfectly natural, the essence of all nature. Science and atheism believe in natural powers, and both scientists and atheists frequently impress me with their spirituality.

[82] In literature, context is the part of a text or statement that surrounds a particular word or passage and determines its meaning. It is also the circumstances in which an event occurs -- a setting, so it is a container or vessel. Its root is a Latin verb that means to weave together. Therefore, a context is a vessel that nurtures and directs the way in which its contents come together.

Chapter Eight

[83] Life coaching is a rapidly growing form of counseling provided by experienced individuals who focus on helping others bring clarity into their lives through a series of telephone interviews. A H.O.P.E. LifeCoach has the specific skills and experience that make SoulCircling possible. For more information, write us or call us. Visit our web site: www.hopelifecoach.com.

[84] Some people stay strictly with the image of a clock face. Some others separate the circle into pie-shaped wedges, varying their widths as they see fit. Some people have completely avoided the use of the clock or pie symbol, using entire landscapes or single trees as the backgrounds for their life's story. Some circles have flowed like water. As SoulCircles are expressions of individuality, they must also be allowed to reflect the character and nature of the individual.

[85] Russell Herman Conwell (1843-1925) coined the phrase, Acres of Diamonds, in 1861. It was the title of a lecture based on the true story of a major diamond discovery in South Africa that he told at least 6,000 times to fund the development of Temple University in 1888. This lawyer, author, clergyman, and educator brought in over $6 million with his story of how a South African farmer became convinced he could find diamonds and sold his farm in order to go prospecting for them. He failed, and drowned himself in his despair...at about the same time that the man who had bought the farm discovered thousands of diamonds in a dry creek bed less than two hundred yards from the farmhouse!

The lecture developed the theme that all of our opportunities and the resources with which to take advantage of them lie in our own backyard waiting for us to discover them. Conwell believed that these diamonds paved the way to success and that each of us has a unique image of what success looks like. He was certain that success came to those who consciously created such an image and steadfastly, carefully moved toward it. Furthermore, Conwell taught that we must use these wonderful resources for nothing but the highest common good. He built Temple University on those principles and it thrives today because of them.

[86] The psychiatrist and Jungian analyst, Jean Shinoda Bolen, wrote two rich books about the Grecian archetypes. She titled the first, *Goddesses in Every Woman* (New York: HarperCollins, 1985), and the second, *Gods in Every Man* (New York: HarperCollins, 1990). She makes it possible for the reader to discover which gods and/or goddesses comprise her or his panoply of archetypes.

[87] Carolyn Myss, Ph.D., has a rich appreciation of these archetypes, and she has developed an in-depth practice that helps a person discover her or his own (*Sacred Contracts*. New York: Harmony, 2002). Native Americans see the behavior of animals as models of human behavior, so the animals are archetypes. Jamie Sams and David Carson' *Medicine Cards* (Santa FE: Bear, 1988) can help you get in touch with your animal archetypes.

[88] A study on goal setting at a major university revealed that only four percent of the incoming freshman class set goals. Twenty-four years later, the class graduates were asked if they considered their lives to be successful. Eighty percent of those who answered "Yes" came from the original four percent who set goals. Their combined income was greater than that of the rest of the class, and their success was not related to their grade point average. The investigators of the class had not studied its spirituality, so we cannot say if soul or ego was behind the goal setting. We could say with confidence that either there were few spiritual people in that class or that egos do not set goals… or both, and is not it sad that people do not have a life-enriching vision.

[89] Assagioli, Roberto, MD. *The Act of Will*. David Platts, 1999, ISBN 0952400413.

[90] When Andrew Carnegie challenged Napoleon Hill to study the lives of the people that Carnegie knew and whom he considered successful, Hill's response was immediate, brilliant, and successful, itself. All of those whom he interviewed had definiteness of purpose, self-discipline, a positive mental attitude. They set goals, reviewed their goals regularly, created masterminds to do the work with them, and compensated them for their work. They all shared the awareness that the success would not have been possible *without the presence of the power greater than themselves.*

[91] American Heritage Dictionary

[92] Andrew Carnegie taught Napoleon Hill the power of affirmation. When he challenged Hill to do the research project on the essence of success by interviewing hundreds of his successful friends, he put out a challenge that tested Hill's confidence to its core: He told Hill that he, Hill, would have to agree to surpass him, Carnegie. Hill could not see how he could surpass the world's first billionaire. Carnegie replied that he did not know *how* Hill was to surpass him, but he reassured Hill that it is in the nature of humans to surpass each other. When Hill agreed to accept Carne-

gie's challenge, he asked how, sensing that Carnegie knew. Carnegie commented that because Hill had to look at himself in the mirror every morning when he shaved, he could look into his eyes then and say, "Napoleon Hill I see you surpassing Andrew Carnegie." He also told Hill that twenty-one repetitions would do it and that Hill was to come back in three weeks and tell about his experience. Hill did as he was told and when he came back, he told Carnegie that he laughed derisively at himself for eleven days, doubted his laughter for the next seven, at which time it made sense, and the next three days were pure gravy. Carnegie was an excellent psychologist and Hill was a superb student.

Epilogue

[93] Boston: Little, Brown and Company, 1985.

[94] Cooper, Rabbi David A., *God is a Verb*. (Riverhead Books; ISBN: 1573220558: September 1997.)

Printed in the United States
1092800005B

9 780972 576000